FUTURE OF WORKPLACE DESIGN

Placemaking for a GenBlend Workforce

ABI RONI MATTOM

STARDOM BOOKS
www.StardomBooks.com

STARDOM BOOKS
112 Bordeaux Ct.
Coppell, TX 75019, USA

Copyright © 2024 by Abi Roni Mattom

This book is copyrighted under the Berne Convention.
No reproduction without permission.
All rights reserved.

The authorship right of Abi Roni Mattom is identified and asserted hereby in accordance with sections 77 and 78 of the Copyright, Designs and Patents Act, 1988.

FIRST EDITION NOVEMBER 2024

STARDOM BOOKS, LLC.
112 Bordeaux Ct. Coppell, TX 75019, USA
www.stardombooks.com
Stardom Books, United States Stardom Alliance, India

The author and publishers have made all reasonable efforts to contact copyright holders for permission and apologize for any omissions or errors in the form of credits given. Corrections may be made to future editions.

Future of Workplace Design
Placemaking for a GenBlend Workforce

Abi Roni Mattom

p. 166
cm. 13.97 X 21.59

Category: ARC011000
Architecture: Buildings-Public, Commercial & Industrial

ISBN: 978-1-957456-58-4

To the unsung heroes of corporate real estate.

The visionary corporate real estate leaders navigating the ever-evolving landscape of business needs and critical missions.

The brokers who bridge the gap between tenants and landlords, fostering creative collaborations.

To the facility managers who build communities by solving everyday workplace challenges and bringing diverse stakeholders together.

To the workplace designers and strategists whose creativity goes beyond aesthetics, delivering design solutions that align with business objectives.

And to the project managers, the conductors who orchestrate the complex symphony of tasks and resources, turning visions of the workplace into reality.

This book is for you.

CONTENTS

	Foreword	i
	Acknowledgments	v
	Introduction	1
1.	Understanding Generations: Unraveling the Workforce Tapestry	5
2.	Key Challenges: Navigating the Complexity of a Multigenerational Workforce	17
3.	Adaptive Workplace for Younger Generations	29
4.	Recalibrating for the Industry	47
5.	Hyper Flexibility and New Ways of Working	61
6.	Move to Practical Wellness: Prioritizing Employee Well-Being in the Workplace	75
7.	All About Flexibility: Embracing Agile Work Environment	99
8.	Embracing the Digital Age in the Workplace	111
9.	Making Offices Futureproof	129
	Conclusion	149
	References	151

FOREWORD

Designing Future-Ready Workplaces:
A Blueprint for the Multi-Generational Workforce

Vikas Kumar, MRICS
Vice President-Asset Management
Tata Realty and Infrastructure Limited

Over the past few years, the commercial real estate industry has undergone a cardinal shift in how offices are designed, created, and managed. There is a pertinent and essential need to create workplaces that are specifically focused on today's multi-generational workforce. This question is particularly relevant in today's socio-economic scenario—as India, Vietnam, Thailand, and many other developing countries look to grow economically and compete globally over the next few decades, our workforce will be the catalyst for this development.

India has the world's largest, growing population at 1.45 billion people. The urban population at ~36% has also increased significantly as more jobs are being created in the cities. The supporting infrastructure is developing rapidly as the real estate markets have become more lucrative. India's urban metro cities are now the favored option for global corporations when setting up offshore 'Capability Centers' and offices. India provides the talent, infrastructure, connectivity, and cost advantages to multinational and Indian corporations. The median age of India's population is low at 28.4 years, and there is an almost urgent need to move away from traditional designs and create workplaces for a much younger and significantly different generation. While the relevance of this timely book to India's growth story is clear, this book holds vital insights into designing effective workplaces for all countries and markets.

In this context, this book delves into concepts of future workplaces that are specially designed with a focus on the multi-generational pool of employees. Abi Roni Mattom, in this book, highlights how workplaces should be created to foster inclusivity, embrace technology, drive collaboration, provide flexibility to work, and yet improve efficiency and retention of top talent. He also calls out that while catering to the new generation of employees, workplaces eventually need to encourage competition and innovation.

A very important aspect of Abi's research highlights the various challenges of working with and creating workplaces specifically designed for today's younger workforce. This younger workforce thinks very differently – Gen Zers are the dreamers of today; they aspire for growth opportunities, fulfillment from work, stability, and flexibility at work. They also want organizations to give back more to society and be sustainable and environmentally friendly. This workforce is more digitally aware and active online on social media and yet craves more personal connections with friends and family. While this transition to a younger workforce is relevant, there are also many employees who are older and have significantly different needs from the workplace. He effectively analyzes solutions aimed at designing relevant workplaces for a dynamic, multi-generational workforce.

Abi's deep insights into the needs of the different workforces are phenomenal. He has assessed the needs of each generation backed by relevant data and insights and supported them with experts' opinions from across the globe. These needs have a direct impact on how today's workplaces should be designed and how they can incorporate elements that ensure the needs of the multi- generational workforce are met effectively. He supports his ideas via case studies and cutting-edge ideas from some of the world's leading organizations like Hewlett Packard and new-age companies like TiVo.

Today, workplaces need to be evolving and yet future-proof. Abi provides insights on how workplaces should be designed to ensure that they are still relevant in the future and cater to the ever-changing needs of the newer generations of the workforce. He highlights the need to future-proof workplaces by driving focus on core concepts like inclusivity, social and environmental responsibility, and, most importantly, the 'human- centric approach.'

Mattom has written this book at a very significant and relevant moment in the timeline of the corporate real estate journey. As our workforce transitions from the Millennials to Gen Z and perhaps the Gen Alpha, the demand for efficient yet effective workplaces for our newer generations becomes increasingly significant. Workplace design must continuously adapt and evolve to ensure that generational talent can be retained and that the workplace effectively promotes productivity, efficiency, creativity, and innovation.

Abi has been a compatriot in the corporate real estate industry for many years. He has an inquisitive mind, and in a relatively traditional and conservative industry, he stands out as a pioneer who understands the needs of the future and always asks pertinent questions relevant to the times we live in in the fast- evolving social and economic fabric of our society. He has written a book that is relevant and sensitive to today's transformational, multi-generational workforce and very important for real estate occupiers and developers, architects, sustainability experts, and anyone else involved in the workplace ecosystem.

Vikas is an army veteran and a thought leader in the corporate real estate industry. He is an expert in Facilities Management, Corporate real estate strategy, and operations. He has 24+ years of experience leading large, transformational teams for occupiers, international property consultants, and real estate developers. He passionately writes about effective leadership, diversity, inclusion, and sustainability in the workplace.

ACKNOWLEDGMENTS

Thank you to the numerous Gen Z, Millennials, and Gen X users who participated in my survey and spoke to me in detail as part of this journey. Your responses will help reshape not just our understanding of the workplace but also of the new generations arriving at it. One of my goals is to ensure your voice is captured!

Thank you, Dr. Reen Salleh, for your invaluable insights and for taking the time to share them with me. I am truly grateful for the opportunity to collaborate with you on various projects. Your vision for the future of work—especially in human-centric design, digital transformation, and immersive technology—is truly inspiring.

I look forward to seeing your ongoing work and thought leadership continue to shape workplaces across the globe. You have been a true inspiration!

Vikas Kumar, I cannot thank you enough for reading and providing feedback on the manuscript, as well as for writing the foreword that encapsulates the essence of this project—despite your busy schedule. Your insights on leadership, diversity, inclusion, and sustainability bring a powerful perspective to this work and beyond.

Thank you, Vikas, for your support and wisdom and for sharing your vision in the foreword.

Tim Larson, thank you for your invaluable contributions. As a thought leader and innovator in digital experiences and experiential design, your insights have greatly enriched this project. Your work in human-environment interaction and forward-thinking approach to generative AI tools have shaped many of the ideas presented here. Thank you, Tim, for sharing your knowledge through our interview and for your ongoing support as a leader and mentor.

Your passion for innovation continues to inspire.

A heartfelt thank you to Sid for your time, expertise, and thoughtful review. Your insights were invaluable, and your attention to detail truly helped elevate this work. I deeply appreciate the effort you put into providing such thorough feedback.

A huge thank you to Krishna for the incredible cover design. Your creativity and vision brought the essence of this book to life in a way that words alone couldn't

I owe a profound debt of gratitude to my partner, Ribu, whose unwavering support and encouragement have been instrumental in the completion of this book. Your patience, understanding, and belief in my work have been a constant source of strength, allowing me to dedicate the time and energy needed to see this project through. This accomplishment is as much yours as it is mine.

Finally, thank you, Raam, Ranjitha, and the team at Stardom. You have an amazing group, and this book would not have happened without you. Thank you for guiding me through the entire process and making every step of the way so enjoyable!

– Abi Roni Mattom

INTRODUCTION

As we approached the second decade of the 2000s, a visible shift emerged in the demographic landscape of workplaces. Older generations began retiring, making way for an influx of younger, more dynamic individuals, particularly those from Generation Z, shaped significantly by the Covid-19 pandemic. This generational transition has created a volatile mix of people, amplifying the potential for both conflict and innovation. Amidst this evolving scenario, the youngest and most technologically adept generation, Gen Z, stands poised to influence and transform the future of work in unprecedented ways.

In the rapidly evolving workplace landscape of the century, the importance of designing safe and healthy environments for employees cannot be overstated. As we witness a paradigm shift in how we perceive and prioritize mental health, it becomes imperative for organizations to address the well-being of their workforce proactively.

Reflecting on workspaces of the past decade, it's evident how employees used to carry the weight of daily stress home with them. The residual effects of this stress, often unnoticed, have lingered and influenced the current generation of employees. While not universal, a significant number of organizations have unwittingly perpetuated this cycle of stress and its detrimental impact on employee well-being.

INTRODUCTION

Traditionally, office environments were characterized by functional yet uninspiring setups—revolving chairs, basic computer tables, and minimal ergonomic considerations. Despite their lack of aesthetic appeal, employees became accustomed to this culture. However, the expectations and standards for office design have since evolved.

Contemporary workplaces are witnessing a transformative shift towards prioritizing employee comfort and health. This shift is manifested in the adoption of better, ergonomic furniture over flimsy ones. These changes not only enhance the physical comfort of employees but also contribute to their overall well-being and productivity.

For professionals entrenched in corporate real estate or organizational leadership roles, this evolution in workplace design presents both challenges and opportunities. Those who are yet to embrace sustainable and inclusive methods risk falling behind in creating environments conducive to employee flourishing.

This book promises to be a game-changer for such individuals, offering comprehensive frameworks to catalyze positive outcomes in their efforts to enhance workplace environments. By embracing these principles, organizations can foster a culture of well-being, productivity, and inclusivity, ultimately transforming the employee experience for the better.

The evolving attitudes towards mental health and personal well-being, particularly among the younger generation, underscore the need for workplaces to prioritize spaces that facilitate relaxation and stress relief. Incorporating open areas within the workspace where employees can unwind and rejuvenate, even during work hours, is essential. Additionally, careful consideration of color palettes can positively impact the mood and productivity of individuals, especially those with conditions like ADHD and OCD, by creating a calming and supportive environment.

The rapid advancements in technology present both challenges and opportunities for organizations seeking to enhance efficiency and alleviate the burdens placed on employees. Integrating technological solutions into the work culture can streamline processes, saving valuable time and reducing the stress associated with manual tasks. Embracing technology not only boosts productivity but also motivates employees to focus on more meaningful and impactful aspects of their roles.

The interplay between different generations within the workforce, coupled with evolving technologies and organizational cultures, has fundamentally transformed the traditional office landscape. Recognizing the diverse perspectives and experiences that employees bring to the table, including those with various conditions, is crucial in fostering inclusivity and understanding within the workplace. Building safe spaces where individuals feel respected and supported encourages collaboration and innovation, enriching the overall work culture. This transformation requires an adaptive approach to workplace design, one that acknowledges the diverse needs and preferences of employees across generations and aligns with the evolving dynamics of work culture.

Within the pages of this book, we embark on a journey through the complexities woven by the multigenerational workforce and its relationship to the physical workspace. Delving into the nuanced needs and preferences of different generations, we uncover how these factors intersect with the ever-changing landscape of work culture. By navigating this maze of intricacies, you can unlock the full potential of your workforce and cultivate environments that inspire creativity, collaboration, and success.

Along with outcomes of detailed research, industry insights, and practical experience, this book offers a comprehensive roadmap for designing adaptive environments that effectively meet the diverse needs of today's workforce. With each chapter meticulously written, you will be guided through a journey of exploration, uncovering strategies and insights to transform their workplaces into thriving hubs of productivity and well-being.

Flexibility lies at the heart of modern workplace design, and this book provides invaluable guidance on creating layouts that adapt to the evolving needs of employees. From agile workstations to

INTRODUCTION

dynamic collaboration spaces, the emphasis is on fostering environments that empower individuals to work in a manner that best suits their preferences and the tasks at hand.

Collaboration is important for propelling innovation and achieving organizational goals, and this book offers practical strategies for fostering a culture of teamwork and synergy. From designing communal areas that inspire spontaneous interactions to implementing virtual collaboration platforms that transcend geographical boundaries, you will learn how to create an environment that facilitates meaningful connections and idea-sharing.

As you delve deeper into each chapter, you will find actionable strategies and inspiring examples that will empower you to transform your workplaces into vibrant, adaptive, and inclusive environments. As the boundaries between work and life continue to blur in today's fast-paced world, the role of the physical workspace has evolved beyond being a mere backdrop for daily operations. It has transformed into a dynamic environment that serves as a strong catalyst for innovation, collaboration, and employee satisfaction. Recognizing this shift in perspective is paramount for organizations looking forward to harnessing the full potential of their most valuable asset—their people.

Ultimately, investing in the physical workspace is an investment towards the success and longevity of the organization. By creating environments that foster innovation, collaboration, and employee satisfaction, organizations can attract and retain top talent, drive productivity and creativity, and position themselves for long-term success in an increasingly fierce marketplace.

I'm sure you may have a lot of questions regarding how to create a futureproof workspace.

Keep reading, and you will find the answers to all your questions!

1
UNDERSTANDING GENERATIONS:
UNRAVELING THE WORKFORCE TAPESTRY

The Workplace Melting Pot: Generations Collide

As we stepped into the second decade of the 21st century, workplaces underwent a subtle but significant transformation. Seasoned professionals who had weathered the dot-com bubble, the rise of smartphones, and the dawn of social media are gradually handing over the reins to a new generation - the Gen Z cohort.

Before the pandemic hit, our work lives often followed a predictable rhythm. We shuffled through office corridors, exchanged pleasantries at the coffee machine, and occasionally grumbled about the photocopier acting up. The generational mix was there, but perhaps we didn't pay it much attention. Baby Boomers, Gen Xers, and Millennials coexisted, each bringing their unique perspectives and work habits.

Then came COVID-19, and suddenly, our routines were upended. Zoom calls replaced conference rooms, and pajamas topped with shirts and an occasional blazer became our unofficial work attire. Amid this upheaval, we started noticing things we hadn't before - the birds outside our windows and the quiet streets devoid of rush-hour traffic. We even developed a newfound appreciation for essentials like toilet paper and a stable Wi-Fi connection.

And there, in the midst of it all, stood Gen Z - the digital natives, the Insta-aficionados, the ones who'd grown up with smartphones as extensions of their hands. Some might stereotype them as rebellious green-haired youths, but that's only part of the story. Gen Z brings more than neon hair to the table; they bring an unfiltered authenticity.

Gen Zers are unafraid to express themselves. They'll dye their hair, wear mismatched socks, and challenge norms. In the workplace, this translates to fresh ideas and a willingness to question the status quo. Yes, they'll mellow out as they step into corporate life, but that renegade spirit won't vanish. It's the same spirit that fuels innovation, disrupts industries, and pushes boundaries.

Gen Z takes their careers seriously, too. They're not here for casual games; they're here to make an impact. Employers who overlook this ambition do so at their own peril.

Yet, many leaders remain oblivious. It's like flying a plane while ignoring the instrument panel—dangerous and ill-advised. We've spent years lumping everyone under 40 as "millennials," but Gen Z is distinct. They're pragmatic, tech-savvy, and hungry for purpose.

So, let's acknowledge it: Gen Z is a force. They're not just "the younger generation." They're the ones who'll shape our future workplaces. It's time to dust off those old handbooks, rethink our strategies, and embrace the blend of ambition, creativity, and independence they bring.

Dear reader, the workplace is evolving, and Gen Z is leading the charge. Let's welcome them, learn from them, and together, rewrite the rules for a better, more innovative tomorrow!

Why is managing a multigenerational workforce challenging?

The delightful clash of generations in the workplace – it's like a never-ending battle of values and expectations. One generation thinks long hours are the key to success like they're in a never-ending episode of "Workaholics," while the other is on a mission to find that mythical unicorn called work-life balance. It's like mixing oil and water – it doesn't quite blend.

So, what's cooking beneath the surface here? It's all about those deep-seated values imprinted on each generation during their formative years. Let's break it down to understand better.

On one side, you've got the "fast and furious" generation. They're all about competition, survival of the fittest, and getting to the finish line at warp speed. It's like their engines are turbocharged for life. To them, long hours are like a badge of honor given to above-average performers because it screams commitment and hard work.

Then, there's the "inclusive and diverse" group of people in the workplace whose mantra is about creating a space for everyone, especially those hanging out at the fringes of society. Inclusion is their favorite mantra. They're not just looking to survive; they want to build a world where everyone gets a seat at the table. But here's the thing – inclusion takes time and is all about collaboration, not cutthroat competition.

Now, you see the dilemma. It's like trying to merge a Ferrari with a cozy minivan. These clashes aren't just surface-level disagreements; they go deep, like an archaeological dig into our belief systems.

Now, instead of letting these clashes tear us apart, what if we saw them as an opportunity? What if we could harness the power of both value systems? It's like mixing a sports car's speed with a minivan's versatility. Imagine the possibilities!

So, next time you find yourself locked in a generational argument at the office, remember that it's not just about who's right or wrong. It's about understanding where these values come from and finding a way to blend them into a harmonious workplace. After all, isn't variety the spice of life?

What do different generations prefer?

Everyone dances to their own tune, but their dance has a harmony. When you work with people of different generations, it is essential to embrace the fact that people of different generations will communicate differently than the current generation. Dealing with Millennials or Gen Xers is similar to dealing with a diplomat. You might even catch them searching for a meeting room for a serious heart-to-heart conversation with colleagues. Meanwhile, Gen Z is more tech-savvy as they prefer to communicate using the world of instant messaging and video calls and use social media very often. They are the ones who like to express themselves using emojis pretty often. So, if your boss sends out emojis to you in their sleep, you are dealing with a Gen Z er.

No matter how different people from one generation communicate from the other, the goal of a harmonious workplace can be achieved if you embrace these differences and design your workplace and culture to support all these communication styles. You will then be able to watch the magic happen.

Generational misconceptions and stereotypes can be like those stubborn stains on your favorite shirt – they mess things up, especially in the workplace. It's like a never-ending game of "Who's the Best Cohort?"

First up is Generation X. You know, those set of people who are often seen as lacking ambition and being as disengaged as a sloth on a rainy day? Well, guess what? They've got a work ethic that could rival a beaver's dam-building skills, and they're as adaptable as chameleons are to their environment. It's just that they need a nudge in the right direction. If you give them some career growth opportunities, let them spread their wings with a bit of autonomy and watch their career take off like a rocket!

Now, let's talk about the millennials. You may have heard rumors of their entitlement and want of instant gratification. But that's not all true. They're searching for meaningful work and a dash of work-life balance. If you give them clear goals, dish out regular feedback like you give candy to your little kid, and let them know their work has a purpose, you'll have a team of motivated go-getters.

Finally, Generation Z! They are the tech-savvy bunch that most people think is glued to their screens 24/7 and can't hold a real conversation. There's a surprise for you – they're all about authentic, direct communication. They might have their noses in their devices, but they value the real deal. So, here's the plan: you can leverage their digital skills for some groundbreaking innovation, drag them out from behind their screens for some good old face-to-face chats, and sprinkle in a bit of guidance on effective communication.

Instead of pointing fingers and clinging to those generational stereotypes, let's celebrate the unique strengths of each cohort.

How is each generation different from another in work-related values or priorities?

Generational values in the workplace are like trying to decode the secret language of office dynamics.
Different generations, different strokes, am I right? Firstly, we've got the Gen Xers. This set of people loves autonomy. They want to spread their wings, fly solo, and make decisions without someone breathing down their necks. It's like giving them the keys to their own little work kingdom. So, if you want to make Gen Xers happy at work, let them do their thing and watch them thrive.

Now, let's talk about those millennials. They're all about purpose and impact, like they're on a quest to save the world, one spreadsheet at a time. They want their work to align with their values and positively contribute to society. They secretly love to think they are the world's superheroes, ready to save everyone from distress in times of need. So, organizations, if you want to keep millennials motivated, show them how their work is making a difference and watch them soar in their professional life.

There are people in every generation with an entrepreneurial spirit. It's like a contagious bug that can bite anyone. People are craving opportunities for entrepreneurship, freelancing, and so on. They like sailing into the sunset of financial freedom. So, organizations, if you want to attract these go-getters, create a space where they can chase their entrepreneurial dreams while still being part of the team.

This discussion reminds me of the workplace potluck we frequently have. Everyone brings different things to the table. It's like a big, diverse family, each member bringing their unique flavor to the workplace potluck. If you embrace the differences, you will get yourself a recipe for success!

What do work-life balance and career development mean for different generations?

For Generation X, it is all about continuous learning. They're like sponges, soaking up knowledge wherever they go. Do you want to keep them happy? Give them access to professional development programs, throw some lateral career opportunities their way, and sprinkle in some skill enhancement. It's like setting up a learning buffet for these folks, and they're ready to feast. And once in a while, don't forget to give healthy toppings of growth mindset and skill diversification - that's their favorite discussion in the workplace.

Coming to the Millennials, they're all about that work-life balance and meaningful work. But they also hunger for growth and learning. They want mentors, coaches, and access to online learning platforms. So, create individualized career development plans for them and toss in some cross-functional experiences for good measure. They'll be your workplace rockstars in no time.

Shining a spotlight on Generation Z, they are like fresh-faced rookies in the workplace, and they have some unique demands. They are the up-and-coming innovators of the workplace. These folks want feedback and skill development at warp speed, and they're eyeing entrepreneurship as if it's the next big thing. Innovation is their middle name. So, if you want to keep them engaged, create an environment that's all about experimentation and learning. And if you can, build them Innovation labs! It's like their playground of creativity.

How do we harness the unique strengths of each generation?

When you've got Gen X, Millennials, Gen Z, and a whole bunch of ideas that they bring to the table, your office can feel like the hottest spot in town. Here are some strategies that organizations can adopt to effectively harness the strengths of each generation, especially from the workplace design standpoint:

First, let's talk about Inclusive Design. We're talking about creating a work environment where people of all ages feel like the rock stars they are. Boomers, Gen Xers, Millennials, and Gen Zers get a front-row seat and a round of applause for their contributions. It's like turning your workplace into a talent show, and everyone's a star. This kind of environment fosters collaboration and open communication across generations. It's like a big, happy family reunion without awkward conversations about your aunt's cat.

Next up is flexibility. Imagine work choices that are as flexible as a yoga instructor doing the limbo. It's like offering a buffet of options for everyone. Whether you're a Gen Xer who wants to work from home or a Millennial who needs flexible hours to chase their dreams, there's a seat at the table for all of you. Now, you can even share a job like splitting a double scoop of ice cream with your colleague! In the post-COVID world, flexibility is the name of the game, accommodating different generational preferences and needs. So, go ahead and offer that buffet of work choices. It's like saying, "Come one, come all, and work the way that suits you best!"

Now, let's dive into Mentorship. Boomers and Gen Xers are the group that has seen it all in the context of success in an organization. They've got all the maps to success and are ready to share their secrets. So, create a special space where they can pass on their unique mantras of success to the younger generation. It's like a knowledge exchange program where the young tech wizards teach the old pros about the latest gadgets, and the experienced folks show them the shortcuts to success. It's a win-win, like a potluck where everyone brings a dish and leaves with a full plate of wisdom and ideas.

Collaborative Technologies, anyone? Imagine your office as a digital carnival of knowledge-sharing. From the tech-savvy Gen Zers to the Gen X and millennials, everyone's chatting and sharing ideas like there's no tomorrow. You've got collaborative tools and tech platforms that make it as easy as pie to connect, learn, and grow together. It's like throwing a digital party where wisdom and ideas burst out like confetti.

Lastly, Purpose-Driven Design. Your office is where you spend a lot of time, so it better have a purpose that drives you. We've learned from the pandemic that having a strong purpose can make employees willingly want to come to the workplace. This applies to all generations. Create spaces that cater to the needs of older workers in strategic roles and spaces that energize younger workers in fast-paced, innovative settings. It's like designing your office to be the ultimate productivity playground where everyone finds their groove.

It's like turning your office into the hottest club in town, and everyone's on the guest list!

How do we effectively engage and motivate employees from different generations?

Say, you're the big leader in charge, the leader of the pack. Managing different generations isn't always a walk in the park, but it's like running a zoo – you've got to understand and appreciate all the different species in your workplace habitat.

First things first, empathy. It's like having a sixth sense but for feelings. Empathy means putting yourself in the shoes of your Gen X, Millennial, and Gen Z colleagues. Imagine being in their world, with their values and expectations. It's like taking a trip to a foreign country and trying to speak the local language. You might not be fluent, but your effort will go a long way.

Flexibility is key, my friend. It's like doing yoga – you've got to be bendy and stretchy. Different generations have different needs and preferences, and you've got to be like a chameleon, adapting to each one. For Gen Xers, they want autonomy and room to spread their wings. It's like giving them a canvas and letting them paint their masterpiece. Millennials crave purpose and growth, so give them clear goals and mentorship. And Gen Z? Well, they're the tech wizards, so let them work their magic and innovate. If you are flexible enough, you will have a team of superheroes with unique superpowers in no time.

Oh, and here's a pro tip: lead by example. Show respect to all generations and treat each employee as an individual. Be fair and equal to all. And if you've got the power to shape your organization, get input from a diverse group. It's like planning the ultimate potluck dinner – everyone brings their dish, and you end up with a feast of ideas.

Give your employees ownership. Let them take the wheel and steer their own projects. It's like handing over the keys to a sports car – they'll feel the adrenaline rush of responsibility. And if you're creating a new office space, mix it up! Create a project community with members from different generations. It's like throwing a party where everyone's invited, and the result is a happy, collaborative, and cross-generational learning space.

Practical techniques for fostering collaboration and teamwork across generations:

Conversations need to be easy and engaging, like chatting with your favorite barista. Inclusive office designs play a big role in setting the vibe and creating a platform to communicate freely, openly, and with purpose.

First up, open and flexible layouts. Imagine your office is like a chameleon – it can change its colors and shape to suit different moods. Your office needs to function like a Swiss Army knife - open floor plans with cozy lounge spaces, meeting pods, and communal work areas. And don't forget the movable furniture and modular elements. It's like playing with building blocks but for grown-ups. You can rearrange them to fit your team's needs, whether a solo project or a full-blown brainstorming session.

Now, let's talk about diverse work zones. Think of your office as a menu with options for everyone. Some folks like it quiet for focused work, so create those zen-like quiet zones. Others thrive in the buzz of collaboration, so design collaborative zones where ideas flow like a coffee shop conversation.

Community spaces are where the magic happens. It's like the common room we saw in Harry Potter's school, Hogwarts. In an office space, this is where the magic happens (in break times).

Employees from different generations can mingle and share their magical insights in a community space. Your office's social hubs include the cafeteria, break rooms, and outdoor spaces.

Technology integration and collaboration tools are your secret weapons. Imagine interactive whiteboards that turn brainstorming into an art form. Digital displays that bring your ideas to life and smart, collaborative tools that are like a virtual meeting room where everyone's invited. Don't forget easy access to tech tools and connectivity – it's like making sure your spaceship has warp speed.

Personalization opportunities are like the cherry-on-top. Let employees lighten up their workspaces with a bit of their own flair. It's like adding a touch of personality to your desk, whether it's a funky plant, a family photo, or a collection of action figures. In the age of hyper-customization, it's the little things that make a big difference.

Centralized amenities are the heart of your office. Coffee stations, printing stations, recreation areas, games corners, and even the random hydration points, as well as shared resources, are like watering holes where employees gather for a quick chat or a caffeine fix.

And don't forget feedback and iteration. Gen Z folks are all about staying in the loop. So, gather feedback from employees of all ages, especially the younger generation, and tweak your workspace design based on their input. It's like fine-tuning your favorite recipe to perfection.

It's a recipe for increased creativity, productivity, and job satisfaction that'll have everyone saying, "I love where I work!"

2

KEY CHALLENGES:
NAVIGATING THE COMPLEXITY OF A MULTIGENERATIONAL WORKFORCE

KEY CHALLENGES

When I walk into my office, I see people of different generations working together towards a common goal. So, the clash of generations in the workplace is like a showdown between the old school and the new school.

There is humor around and sprinkles of wisdom all over that gets passed on from generation to generation. The older generation loves to burn the midnight oil, working those long hours like a marathon. To them, long hours equal hard work and commitment. It's like they're in a never-ending race to prove their dedication. Let me be clear—this isn't a criticism. I can hand-on-heart say that's just who we are. Meanwhile, the other generation is more inclined to look for an outstanding work-life balance, and they like to hold it like a banner wherever they can, just like it's a victory banner.

They picture life as one delicious pie, and work is just one slice of the life pie, and they want a big, juicy slice of everything else. They're the masters of multitasking, balancing work, family, and personal time. You might have the impression that the new generation doesn't have many expectations from life. But that's wrong. Because here's the juicy part – these expectations come from deep within and are like the hidden ingredient of our beliefs.

One group (Millennial or Gen X) values speed and competition like they're sprinting towards the finish line in a race for survival. It's like they've got turbo boosters strapped to their shoes.

On the flip side, the other group (Gen Z) believes in diversity and inclusion, like they're building a big, inclusive tent for everyone, especially those on the fringes of society. They're not just looking to survive; they want to thrive as a more inclusive society. They are taking their sweet time to ensure no one gets left behind.

Have you ever juggled flaming torches? It's a tricky thing that can turn dangerous if it is not done correctly. Managing a multigenerational workforce can be more challenging than juggling flaming torches. However, some strategies can cool down the process and make it easy.

First up, communication styles and collaboration. Generations might speak different workplace languages, but we can all learn to speak "office-ese." Encourage open communication and offer training on how to bridge the generation gap. When you're designing the workplace, make sure there are spaces where different communication styles can coexist, like those cool immersion rooms with hi-tech AV, interactive screens, and tech and old-school writing boards. It's like creating a playground where everyone can have fun in their way.

Next is knowledge transfer. It's like passing the torch from generation to generation without any Olympic pressure. Establish mentorship programs where the seasoned pros can share their wisdom with the rookies and capture all that institutional knowledge through documentation and training sessions. And how about setting up a library space where any employee can come and seek mentorship or solutions beyond the boundaries of their team or department? It's like having a library card to succeed.

I recently met my friend Suhas for a cup of coffee. He recently got a job at a reputed MNC and was excited to tell me how his first week was, how his new colleagues were, and how the cafeteria food was. I thought he would rant about his manager being strict with him.

But I was pleasantly surprised when he told me, "Abi, what I like best is how senior colleagues handhold their juniors. Training periods are the best!" That got me thinking- "Wow, this is great!"

I have known Suhas for a long time, and he hated attending classes when he was in school. He used to look for the slightest chance of getting punished and sent out of the classroom so he could take a walk on the school grounds.

Now, he is listening to his senior and taking notes. So, mentorship programs do set it up for the next generation. The little sprinkles of wisdom get imbibed into the mind so they can get better and do better every day.

So, if you are a workplace warrior like most of us, embrace the clash of generations with open arms, a willingness to learn, and a sprinkle of flexibility. It's like mixing different ingredients to create the perfect workplace recipe.

The communication style of someone from Gen X differs from that of Gen Z.

How do generational differences impact communication styles?

Hieroglyphics is one of the most ancient communication styles, but it is also very difficult to decode. Sometimes, solving the differences between the communication styles of Gen X and Gen Z is similar to that. So, here we are, in one corner, we've got the "Formal Communicators." They're all about the official channels, the holy trinity of communication: emails, official message boards like Teams and Slack, and the face-to-face meetings that require you to wear your fancy pants. These folks trust communication only if it comes with a stamp of authority.

And then, in the opposite corner, we've got the "Informal Communicators." They're the rebels of the communication world. They wouldn't trust a formal message if it came with a bag of gold. For them, anything from authority is just propaganda. They rely on peer-level reviews and the grapevine of gossip for their daily dose of info. It's like they're navigating a jungle of information and having their tribe guide them.

Now, these differences run deep, my friends. Changing these beliefs is like convincing a cat to take swimming lessons – it won't happen.

But one thing works like a charm across generations – transparency and openness. It's like the universal language of trust. When you're transparent and open in your communication, you're handing out trust cookies to everyone.

From a workplace perspective, let's talk about Gen Z. These folks are the kings and queens of instant messaging, social media, and video calls. They practically breathe in emojis and gifs. Organizations must embrace this and create a workplace supporting their digital communication needs. It's like building a digital playground where they can slide into conversations and bounce ideas off each other like ping-pong balls. On the other hand, Millennials and Gen Xers are like old-school communicators. They're comfortable with emails, phone calls, and good old face-to-face chats. You wouldn't be surprised if they start hunting for a meeting room whenever they need a serious conversation.

So, here's the golden rule – adapt and conquer. By acknowledging and respecting these generational differences in communication, organizations can create a workplace where everyone can speak their communication language. And that, my friends, leads to improved collaboration and understanding and a workplace like a symphony of different voices harmonizing.

The Gen Xers and Millennials have different work expectations. So, let's break it down by generations. What do employees want? Well, it turns out each generation has its Wishlist:

(Generation sense-check source: Purdue University Global)

Baby Boomers (1946-1964):
- They're all about that optimism, like a glass-half-full crew.
- They love the mentorship game, passing down their wisdom like a torch.
- Strong work ethics are their jam; they're like the workhorses of the workplace.
- They dig loyalty, wanting to stick with an employer for the long haul.
- Hierarchy? Yep, they're cool with that. They thrive in a structured setup.
- They crave the chance to mentor others, passing on their knowledge.
- Respect is their currency; they want it and give it in spades.

Gen X (1965-1980):
- These folks are all about independence and doing their own thing.

- Innovation is their middle name; they're always looking for new ways to do stuff.
- Strong communicators can talk the talk and walk the walk.
- Trustworthiness in an employer is critical; they want someone they can rely on.
- Problem-solving opportunities? Bring them on. They love a good challenge.
- Competent colleagues are their kind of folks; they want to be surrounded by the best.
- Autonomy, please. They like making their own decisions.

Millennials (1981-2000):
- Tech-savvy is an understatement; they practically invented the digital age, earning themselves the name 'Digital Immigrants.'
- Collaboration is their game; they're all about working together for the greater good.
- Empathy is their superpower; they want an employer who cares.
- Meaningful work is the goal; they want to make a difference.
- Training for new skills? They're lifelong learners.
- Flexibility in their work arrangements is necessary; they want to balance work and life.

Gen Z (2001-2020):
- Digitally fluent, these digital natives are like the wizards of the internet.
- Practicality is their middle name; they want stuff that works.
- They thrive in diverse workforces, valuing different perspectives.
- Cultural competence in an employer matters; they want diversity and inclusion.
- Competitive wages are a must; they know their worth.
- Mentorship is essential; they want guidance from the pros.

- Stability in their job is critical; they're not fans of constant changes.

Gen Alpha (yet to enter the workplace):
They are perhaps not at the workplace yet, but looking at what makes them different would be interesting.

- **Tech-Savvy:** Generation Alpha has been incredibly comfortable with technology from a very young age, growing up in a highly digitized world. They are likely to be adept at using various digital devices and platforms.
- **Global Awareness:** With access to the internet and social media, Generation Alpha is more globally connected and aware than any previous generation at their age. They are likely to have a broader perspective on world events and cultures.
- **Entrepreneurial Spirit:** Raised in a time of rapid innovation and change, Generation Alpha may exhibit entrepreneurial tendencies and a willingness to take risks in their careers.
- **Individuality and Diversity:** Generation Alpha is growing up in a world that increasingly values diversity and inclusivity. They may be more accepting of differences in ethnicity, gender, sexuality, and other aspects of identity.
- **Environmental Consciousness:** With an increased awareness of environmental issues, Gen Alpha may be more environmentally conscious and inclined towards sustainable practices.
- **Flexible and Adaptive:** Given the pace of technological change, Generation Alpha may be more adaptable and comfortable with uncertainty than previous generations. They may be open to new ideas and ways of working.
- **Parental Influence:** Generation Alpha is often heavily influenced by their parents, who are typically millennials or late members of Generation X. This influence may shape their values, attitudes, and behaviors.

KEY CHALLENGES

According to Dr. Bourne, an expert on generational differences, the characteristics of a generational workforce are distinct from traditional generational labels. Dr. Bourne defines the Millennial workforce as individuals born between 1981 and 2000 and the Generation Z workforce as those born between 2001 and 2020. However, these distinctions do not change the fundamental principles of creating inclusive, genblend workplaces.

As per her, the millennial generation, born between 1981 and 2000, is known for its competitive nature, civic-mindedness, and open-mindedness. Shaped by significant events such as the Columbine High School Massacre and 9/11 tragedies, as well as the rise of the internet, millennials are motivated by responsibility, quality management, and unique work experiences. Their preferred communication style includes instant messages, texts, and email. They seek challenges, growth, development, and a work-life balance and are likely to pursue new opportunities if they encounter resistance to change in their current organization.

Additionally, statistics show that by 2025, 75% of the global workforce will be made up of millennials. Interestingly, 18% of millennial men ages 25–34 live at home with their parents, while 12% of millennial women in the same age group do the same.

On the other hand, Generation Z, born between 2001 and 2020, is characterized as global, entrepreneurial, and progressive, with less focus compared to millennials. Shaped by events like life after 9/11 and the Great Recession, along with early exposure to technology, Generation Z is motivated by diversity, personalization, individuality, and creativity. They prefer to communicate through social media, texts, and instant messages.

The worldview of Generation Z involves self-identifying as digital device addicts, valuing independence and individuality, and favoring working with millennial managers, innovative coworkers, and new technologies.

Relevant statistics indicate that 67% of Gen Zers want to work at companies where they can learn skills to advance their careers, while 80% believe that government and employers should subsidize, pay full tuition, or provide direct training for students.

Leading a multigenerational team is like organizing a family reunion with a really wide range of relatives, each with their own share of unique perspectives and experiences– an adventure that can be interesting if everyone, or most of them, is catered to properly! Let me share with you a few time-tested tips that I have used to navigate this diverse bunch:

Firstly, it's important to unconditionally accept people from all the different generations. Just like at a potluck dinner where everyone brings a different dish, we may not love every dish, but we can appreciate the variety. Embrace the differences without picking favorites.

Secondly, creating a safe space for dialogue is crucial. Just like the dinner table can be a safe place for open conversation, we should create a similar space in the workplace for employees of different generations to express themselves. This fosters trust and respect among team members.

Additionally, situational leadership is important. Adapting your leadership style to fit the situation is crucial when managing a multigenerational team. It's like choosing the right dessert for the occasion - sometimes you need a cake, sometimes pie. Similarly, adapt your leadership style based on what the situation demands. This adaptability empowers you to handle any situation effectively, making you a capable and confident leader.

Moreover, creating a Culture of Inclusivity is essential for a leader. This means making every team member feel valued, respected, and included, regardless of their age or background. To do this, you can encourage open communication, provide equal opportunities for growth, and celebrate diversity. Think of it as setting up a game night where everyone's favorite game gets played. Ensure every voice is heard, especially the more reserved ones. This promotes diversity and inclusion in the workplace. Many successful organizations, such as TCS, Google, GE, and Accenture, implement these strategies to manage a multigenerational workforce.

Lastly, your role in navigating a multigenerational team is like that of a juggler in a variety show. Embracing diversity and ensuring everyone's acts get a chance in the spotlight is paramount. So, lead with humor, flexibility, and a dash of understanding. These qualities not only make your leadership style unique but also inspire and motivate your team. With these tools, your leadership will be the hit of the reunion!

Develop Mentorship Programs: Create structured mentorship initiatives designed to pair employees of varying generations. Encourage active participation where individuals exchange their diverse experiences, perspectives, and insights. Through fostering open and respectful dialogues, employees can cultivate a deeper understanding of one another's viewpoints, ultimately bridging the gap between generations.

Leverage Technology for Learning: Recognize the proficiency of younger generations in technology and promote their involvement in teaching older colleagues. Encourage them to share their expertise in digital platforms, social media, and other technological tools. Facilitating this exchange of knowledge fosters effective communication and cultivates a collaborative learning atmosphere within the workplace.

Foster Cross-Generational Collaboration: Enhance relationships and communication by establishing opportunities for collaboration across age groups. Consider these strategies:

a. **Cross-Functional Teams:** Create teams comprising members from diverse generations and functions. This approach fosters collaboration, exposes individuals to varied work styles, and promotes open communication.
b. **Team-Building Activities:** Plan activities like workshops, group discussions, or social events to facilitate interaction and understanding among different generations. These initiatives provide a relaxed environment for employees to connect and build relationships beyond their regular tasks.

c. **Knowledge-Sharing Platforms:** Implement internal forums or platforms where employees can exchange knowledge, experiences, and insights. These platforms encourage learning from one another and facilitate open dialogue and collaboration across generations.

Organizations can enhance understanding and collaboration by harnessing generational differences, ultimately fostering success and growth. Moreover, leaders can promote inclusivity by demonstrating a genuine willingness to listen to individuals and understand their needs. Rather than imposing mandates, leaders can offer choices, empowering employees to thrive in the evolving workplace.

Adapting to and appreciating these differences is essential for leaders to achieve organizational objectives and cultivate a prosperous future. Embracing diversity and fostering an inclusive environment not only enhances team dynamics but also drives innovation and overall organizational performance.

As we continue our exploration of workplace dynamics, the next chapter will focus on designing the post-pandemic workplace for a new normal, considering the shift in work patterns and the impact of the pandemic on the modern workplace.

Are you ready to dive into the future of work?

3
ADAPTIVE WORKPLACE
FOR YOUNGER GENERATIONS

ADAPTIVE WORKPLACE FOR YOUNGER GENERATIONS

I like to think of the workplace as a diverse garden with various types of flowers – roses, tulips, daisies, and sunflowers. Different generations and personalities add unique colors and fragrances to this garden. Currently, the leadership positions are mainly held by millennials and a few Gen Xers, but in the near future, we have a growing number of Gen Z employees joining the team. To create a harmonious and inclusive environment, we need to consider the needs and preferences of these new entrants.

I recently had the opportunity to dive deep into this subject with a leader while designing a brand-new space for their large workforce. We began thinking about what the effects of a non-inclusive workplace are. And that threw us in a loop. It's like the Bermuda Triangle of offices – people vanishing into a black hole of unproductivity.

We found out that feeling left out makes employees 25% less productive. It's like a never-ending coffee break; they won't lift a finger for the team. Humans crave that warm, fuzzy feeling of belonging, and when they don't get it, they go entire hermit crab – hiding ideas and feedback. And that's a diversity disaster.

My client, the leader, was nodding like, "Yeah, this is my worst nightmare." To top it off, they're moving to a new office, but it's not all rainbows brought about by change management. A catch to this brought about the expression of 'Ouch' from the employees. Longer commutes – an extra 30 minutes in traffic. But there was a silver lining to this cloud. We decided to give a makeover to the new place and make it scream inclusivity. It was a fantastic opportunity when you were moving to a new office, so we brainstormed about how workplace design could influence inclusivity, especially for a sizeable divergent group of people.

The gem we unearthed from the discussion was that the secret sauce to team success isn't just talent or genius IQs. It is all about feeling safe in your team. Without that warm fuzzy feeling, creativity nosedives. So, we're envisioning a space that's a love fest of social connections. Impromptu meetings happen like magic –belonging is more than just being cubicle buddies; it's about being real-life friends. Another concept we developed was spaces and opportunities for people to create art and form at work (like Picasso meets the office copier). We're giving everyone a canvas for their geniuses, especially the quiet ones. To us, the workplace is the place to vibe with every brain type, every gender, and every state of mind. We had to break the mold of all systems and provisions for standard 9- 6 employees and flip the script.

Welcome to the clash of Ergonomic chairs and Nostalgia!

A workplace isn't just desks and coffee machines. An office is a harmonious place of inclusivity, creativity, and cool vibes. Who says office talk can't be this exciting? This always reminds me of the movie Avengers- the characters are diverse, influential, and ready to conquer. A workplace needs to be like that.

The workplace game is changing, and it's not just about having a comfy chair and a stable Wi-Fi connection anymore. Millennials and Gen Z are rewriting the rules. It's not about the corner office or climbing the corporate ladder; it's about learning, growing, and feeling like they belong somewhere.

Think about it – these folks aren't just looking for a desk in a sea of cubicles. They want a space that screams innovation, collaboration, and a bit of that entrepreneurial vibe. The whole 9-to-5 routine is so last century for them. Flexibility is the name of the game, thanks to the gig economy and, of course, the curveball that was the COVID-19 pandemic.

So, when we're discussing designing a workspace for these young guns, it's not just about how many desks fit into a room or where the coffee machine goes. It's about creating an environment where their creative juices can flow freely. Touchscreens for info-sharing, coffee bars, and flexible furniture – that's the language they understand.

ADAPTIVE WORKPLACE FOR YOUNGER GENERATIONS

Flexible work policies: According to a LinkedIn survey, 72% of Gen Z are most likely to leave a job if their employer doesn't offer flexible work policies. Source: Queros.com

- **Transparency and honesty:** 81% of Gen Zers value transparency and honesty in the workplace. (Source: cake.com)
- **Professional development:** 65% of Gen Z are eager for professional development and career growth. (Source: Udemy)
- **Connection with peers and managers:** 29% of Gen Z say they feel connected to their peers and managers through chat messages. (Source: Jabra)
- **Importance of honesty and integrity:** Gen Z employees consider honesty and integrity in a manager to be five times more important than their expertise in a given field.
- **Learning culture:** Gen Z values continuous improvement, and employers who facilitate learning can enhance their capabilities and adaptability. (Source: Remoto Workforce)
- **Unclear or unequal policies:** Unclear or unequal policies can breed resentment, envy, and feelings of inadequacy and exclusion. (Source: Forbes)

It's not a one-size-fits-all situation. You can't just throw in a ping-pong table and call it a day. You must engage with these guys, understand what makes them tick, and tailor the workspace accordingly. It's like designing a custom suit – you wouldn't assume everyone fits the same size. There is an ongoing myth that the new generation of individuals is all about being glued to their screens. Don't buy into that myth. They take their work seriously and want a workspace that reflects that. So, the next time you brainstorm a new office layout, think beyond the black and white. Add a splash of hospitality and co-working vibes. It's not just about the paycheck; it's about feeling at home in the workplace, where ideas can collide and bounce around like a game of intellectual pinball.

In a nutshell, it's time to ditch the old-school approach and embrace the new wave. The younger generation is all about customization, so let's give them a space to work, play, and maybe even change the world – one cool office at a time.

Contrary to common beliefs, recent research from one of the workplace design firms shows that younger generations prioritize learning from others face to face. So, that is like a truth bomb shaking up the whole remote work narrative. And, despite current technology, nothing can replace the sense of belonging that in-person interaction provides.

The survey found that employees are both happy to work from home (by settling for lower pay) and to return to the office. How do we balance this contradiction?

The findings truly underscore a fascinating and somewhat contradictory aspect of the employees' attitudes toward working remotely or from the office. On the one hand, employees express contentment with the option to work from home, even willing to accept lower pay for this privilege. On the other hand, there is a willingness and desire to return to the office environment. Navigating this apparent paradox requires a nuanced and adaptable approach that acknowledges and addresses the diverse needs and preferences of the workforce.

Many employers uphold the belief that fostering collaborative environments in the workplace enhances productivity. Their perspective often revolves around the notion that any decline in individual output within the office is offset by the gains achieved through collaboration. However, it is crucial to acknowledge that what employers truly aspire for is not merely increased collaboration but rather more effective collaboration with a distinct purpose.

The office is not in competition with remote work; rather, it contends with the advantages presented by remote work. Most workplaces still adhere to outdated neighborhood models, where workstations are encircled by conference rooms. These spaces were initially designed to accommodate various behaviors, ranging from focused work to collaboration, learning, and socialization. However, in practice, they fail to excel in any of these aspects. The neighborhood concept often results in noise and distractions, which contributes to employees' reluctance to work in the office. When one needs to engage in concentrated or private tasks, sitting at a workstation becomes undesirable.

From our perspective, the traditional neighborhood model is challenged, at the least, and it is gradually giving way to zoning approaches tailored to specific needs. These areas are divided into three categories: "me," "we," and "us" spaces. "Me" spaces encompass personal and focused work environments like pods, phone booths, and small private rooms. "We" spaces encompass areas designed for small group collaboration, such as meeting rooms and collaborative spaces. "Us" spaces encompass relaxed settings like lounges and cafes, offering diverse seating options and fostering connections among colleagues. Providing this array of spaces aims to mirror and amplify the flexibility and autonomy that employees enjoy while working remotely from anywhere.

Other key observations from the survey that are particularly relevant for Indian companies were as follows:

India has probably the world's largest young workforce, and a significant proportion of them either started their careers or were in the early years of their career when the pandemic forced everyone to work remotely.

While the flexibility of remote work is appreciated by them, employers should also pay heed to a stunning finding from the survey that a substantial 59% of the surveyed employees indicate they are grappling with burnout due to excessive workloads and a feeling that they need to always be online, or constantly prove to their manager that they are online when working from home.

This highlights the urgency for businesses to implement strategies that foster a healthier work-life balance.

There is also a troubling disconnect between employers and employees regarding career progression in a hybrid work scenario.

84% of employers surveyed believe that regular office attendance is essential for career advancement, whereas only 67% of employees share this perspective.

This dissonance underscores a critical challenge in aligning expectations and perceptions between employers and their workforce. If a significant proportion of employers continues to perceive in-person presence as crucial for career progression, it could inadvertently disadvantage those who thrive in remote or hybrid work settings.

Bridging this gap requires a reevaluation of traditional notions of career development and emphasizing skills, performance, and contributions over physical presence. Companies must recognize that the hybrid work model necessitates a paradigm shift in how success and career advancement are defined and create clear and objective criteria for appraisals that emphasize results, innovation, and adaptability rather than physical presence.

While younger workers typically have access to technology and the technical skills required to work remotely for an extended period, studies indicate that this age group values the opportunity, cooperation, and support that a physical office gives more than any other. This is shocking, right?

My experience with a leading product and technology firm

I recently worked for a leading product and technology firm's regional HQ. We created a design that integrates a digital experience layer throughout, creating a seamless digital experience and fostering an interactive environment for a diverse workforce. It's like stepping into the future but with really cool furniture. The design solution introduced "stimulants" to tap into unused potential and align with the firm's work style.

Technology was critical in activating areas, particularly the Immersive spaces in the living studio, which enable touch, view, and interaction with presented material. Collaborative workplaces are aided by technologically advanced stimulating spaces, such as the multi-purpose room with movable screens and customizable walls. The environment is built for intensive brainstorming sessions, with various seating sections, tables, writing surfaces, and strategically positioned screens. Informal discussions are encouraged in locations such as the work café, which is equipped with technology to function as both a cafe and a workspace.

It's not your average coffee corner; it's a tech-infused chill zone where informal chats are as welcome as a strong espresso. Double duty, you see?

More recently, I was in conversation with Dr. Reen Salleh, the head of Workplace Strategy, Planning & Experience in the Asia Pacific and Japan (APJ) region for HP Inc. She boasts an impressive career spanning over two decades in the corporate real estate industry, which is marked by her expertise in various disciplines, including workplace/portfolio transformation and strategy, workplace experiential design, and change management. I also had the opportunity to dig deeper into what her organization is doing right in terms of space design and employee productivity.

Throughout her career, Reen has successfully delivered numerous complex projects, including offices, R&D and Manufacturing facilities, and campuses, both for HP Inc. in the APJ region and previously for major multinational corporations across Asia. Our conversation really put things into perspective, and I was able to collect some really insightful data:

1. How has HP Inc. prioritized employee well-being and contributed to overall organizational success?

Unhealthy relationships with work significantly impact employees' mental, emotional, and physical well-being, which in turn affects business performance.

Some of the key points to note include:

Morale and Engagement:	Poor work relationships lead to lower productivity, higher disengagement, and increased feelings of disconnection.
Retention:	Neutral feelings about work make employees consider leaving, with a higher likelihood for those who are unhappy.
Mental Well-being:	Struggles with work relationships result in low self-esteem and feelings of failure.
Emotional Well-being:	Personal relationships suffer, and employees feel too drained to pursue personal passions.
Maintaining healthy eating, exercise, and sleep routines becomes difficult due to poor mental and emotional wellness.	

These points underscore the need to improve employees' relationships with work to enhance overall well-being and business outcomes. Employees' expectations of work have evolved significantly in the past two to three years, with most employees acknowledging these changes.

Some key findings include:

Fulfillment:	Employees seek purpose, empowerment, and connection in their work, but few experience these consistently. Businesses must prioritize employee fulfillment by increasing their voice and agency.

Leadership:	While most business leaders recognize the need for new leadership styles, few employees feel leaders have adapted. Emotional intelligence and transparent, empathetic leadership are crucial.
People-centricity:	Few knowledge workers feel respected and valued, experiencing the desired flexibility, autonomy, and work-life balance. Leaders should put people first and involve teams in decision-making.
Skills:	Most knowledge workers value strong technical skills, but some lack confidence in their proficiency. Investing in holistic training and support offers businesses an edge in skills development and employee engagement.
Tools:	Employees want input into the technology their employers provide, seeking inclusive tools that support hybrid work. Effective technology is essential for employee engagement and connection.
Workspace:	Knowledge workers desire a seamless experience between work locations and the choice of where to work each day. Effective hybrid workspaces, easy transitions, and autonomy foster trust and a positive work experience.

This pivotal time offers an opportunity to redefine work relationships, with trust and emotional connection being key themes. Almost three in four business leaders acknowledge that emotionally intelligent leadership is essential for future success. Notably, emotional intelligence and increased trust and agency are highly valued by employees.

Prioritizing employee well-being is a strategic investment that yields significant benefits for both employees and the organization as a whole. Organizations that have implemented well-being initiatives report various positive outcomes, including:

Reduced Absenteeism:	Healthier, happier employees are less likely to take sick leave, leading to fewer disruptions and more consistent productivity.
Increased Employee Satisfaction:	Well-being programs often lead to higher employee satisfaction scores, reflecting a more positive work experience.
Higher Engagement Scores:	Organizations that focus on well-being typically see improvements in employee engagement metrics, indicating that employees are more invested in their work.
Better Health Outcomes:	Companies that offer health and wellness programs often see improvements in employees' physical health, which can reduce healthcare costs and improve overall workplace morale.

2. **How does the younger generation perceive or react to overall wellness measures at the workplace?**

The younger generation in organizations often perceives and reacts to workplace wellness measures positively and with high expectations. The younger generation in organizations is generally receptive and appreciative of workplace wellness measures. They value a holistic approach to well-being and expect flexibility, inclusivity, and continuous improvement in wellness initiatives. Meeting these expectations can lead to higher engagement, retention, and overall positive outcomes for the organization.

Exploding topics recently reported less than 1 in 5 among the older contingent of Gen Z would say they are very happy. While 40% of Gen Z report these mental health struggles.

Some key observations include:

Positive acceptance: Younger employees tend to place a high value on mental, emotional, and physical well-being, seeing it as a fundamental aspect of a desirable workplace. They appreciate organizations that prioritize wellness, often regarding such initiatives as essential rather than optional. This demographic is generally more engaged with wellness programs, actively participating in initiatives like mental health workshops, fitness challenges, and flexible working arrangements. Moreover, they are strong advocates for better wellness measures, pushing for improvements if existing programs fall short. Vocal about their needs, younger employees expect employers to respond accordingly, demonstrating a commitment to creating a supportive and healthy work environment.

Expectation and response: They also expect a holistic approach to wellness that encompasses not only physical health but also mental health support, work-life balance, and personal development opportunities. They highly value flexibility in how, when, and where they work, finding wellness programs that offer options for remote work, flexible hours, and autonomy particularly appealing. Additionally, they appreciate the use of modern technology and inclusive tools that support hybrid work environments, anticipating seamless digital experiences that enhance their work-life integration. This generation also expects continuous improvement in wellness measures, with regular updates to programs based on feedback. They value organizations that proactively adapt to their evolving needs, demonstrating a commitment to their overall well-being.

Observe Trends include Organizations that prioritize wellness tend to attract and retain younger talent more effectively, as young employees are likely to stay longer with companies that demonstrate a genuine commitment to their well-being. This emphasis on wellness leads to higher engagement and productivity, with younger employees feeling more motivated and invested in their work. They are more likely to contribute positively to the organization and actively participate in company culture. Furthermore, wellness measures help create a positive and supportive work environment, which is crucial for younger employees. They thrive in settings where they feel cared for and supported, leading to overall improved organizational performance and employee satisfaction.

Challenges: The high expectations of younger employees can be challenging for organizations to meet consistently, requiring companies to be agile and responsive to feedback to maintain high levels of satisfaction. This generation's diverse needs add another layer of complexity, as their wellness requirements can vary widely. Organizations must ensure their wellness programs are inclusive and adaptable, catering to different preferences and lifestyles. By acknowledging and addressing these varied needs, companies can create a supportive environment that resonates with younger employees, fostering loyalty and engagement.

3. **Some examples of digital tools and solutions that can enhance the workplace experience.**

These digital tools and solutions can greatly enhance the workplace experience by improving communication, collaboration, productivity, well-being, and continuous learning.

Communication & Collaboration	
Microsoft Teams	A collaboration platform that integrates with Office 365, allowing for chat, video meetings, file storage – one drive or SharePoint, and application integration.
Zoom	A video conferencing tool that supports virtual meetings, webinars, and breakout rooms, making remote communication seamless.
Engage	Desk reservation system to enable employees to go to the right location to collaborate and navigate in different office settings.

Wellness & Employee Engagement	
Virgin Pulse	A platform that promotes employee wellness through personalized wellness journeys, challenges, and health tracking.

Learning & Development	
Brain Candy	It serves as a delightful way to expand knowledge or explore new ideas. It's a valuable tool for engaging the mind and promoting lifelong learning in a relaxed and enjoyable manner.
In-house learning and development tools and continuous collaboration among employees through interest group engagement, volunteering programs, and benefits.	

The Saga of Technology and Gen Z

Innovative technologies, from AI to robotics, continue to shape and disrupt how we work. It's like they are doing the cha-cha with how we work. It all looks great, but too much tech love can cause our concentration to shambles.

According to a Hubble survey, 77% of Gen Z employees want their company to have an office, which is higher than the average of 70.5% across all generations. – both for impromptu gatherings with their colleagues and for some quiet solo work. It's like they're craving the perfect work playlist!

This presents a huge opportunity to better support Gen Z by reassessing how office space is designed and utilized. The game plan to prepare today's workspaces must ride the tech wave while recognizing humans aren't machines. We can address these challenges at the office by designing common spaces that are intentionally low-tech, encouraging face-to-face interaction, and providing quiet environments where employees may relax and recharge.

The greenery (biophilia) is also essential in the workplace. One-third of our lives are spent at work, mostly indoors for office dwellers. So, why not sprinkle in some greenery? Plants, water features, natural materials –like an office spa day.

Studies say it reduces stress, amps up brainpower, and boosts creativity. It's like the office saying, "Hey, we care about your sanity." or "Hey, let's create spaces where tech takes a chill pill." They are creating low-tech communal areas that promote face-to-face interaction – and for those moments when you need a breather, there should be private spots where you can just Zen out and recharge. So, in a nutshell, technology is cool, but let's not drown in it. It's time to dial down the interruptions, find our work beat, and maybe, just maybe, throw in a potted plant or two for good measure.

Are Gen Z potential decision-makers?

A study recently revealed that Gen Z's decision journey cycle is fluid. Gen Z's decision cycle starts and ends with self-reflection, and in between, they rely on personal advisors, online research, and, to some extent, AI tools to make informed choices. So, their decision-making journey is like a roller coaster.

Now, imagine you're a designer or someone providing workplace services. You've got to treat Gen Z like the VIP client within the client squad. They're not just nodding along; they're informed decision-makers.

With all the info they've got and their craving for influence and FOMO (Fear of Missing Out), you better believe they want a say in the game. I wouldn't be surprised if the younger generation soon comes up with a clear design brief on how they want their office or workplace designed, how they imagine the office layout, and what finishes they would like to see in their new place!

ADAPTIVE WORKPLACE FOR YOUNGER GENERATIONS

They stroll into the office like, "Here's how I want my workspace to look; this is the layout, and these are the finishes I need." Boom! They've got their vision board ready for the office makeover.

The future of office design might be in the hands of the ones who know what they want and want it crystal clear.

As bizarre as every individual is perceived differently at the workplace, your perception and reality significantly impact your behavior, don't you agree? People from different generations, industries, and roles, as well as men and women, see the workplace differently. It's like different strokes for different folks, especially regarding industries and roles.

For starters, let's look at how the designs vary between industries. Let's start with the digital and marketing scene first. Picture this: open spaces, team desks for days, and collaboration vibes in the air. Meetings are a big deal, with the serious one's going down in private rooms and the more chill ones happening in cozy pods. And if your boss is all about that work-life balance, you might spot neon beanbags or those fancy sleep pods. Napping on the job – what a concept!

Now, swing over to an offshore development center (ODC) or even the talk of the town, GCCs (The Global Capability Centers,) which has attracted a lot of Indian talent, apparently making up a whopping 30% of India's employee base. It's like a sea of workstations, almost like they're in their little fortresses.

Privacy is key, and meeting rooms? Let's say they're more about one-on-one calls or tiny pods for those quick brainstorming sessions. Then again, we have law firms being set up with the Bar Council relaxing rules for foreign firms on Indian soil, which could be a potential area of growth in the near future; lawyers are on a whole different wavelength.

They're not hopping on the hybrid workplace train anytime soon. Private offices are what they like and give a hard pass to shared spaces.

Shared space is unappealing for those who work on sensitive material and spend most of their time in heads-down concentration or on private calls with clients, judges, and fellow lawyers. Venture capital firms express almost the same sentiments.

It's like young engineers and analysts rule the roost. Lastly, the startup vibe of warm lights and cozy sofas is distinct and mostly promising for younger employees and future founders.

Now, when it comes to roles, it's like a chessboard. HR people are all about privacy and storage – the front-and-center action. Managers? They're eyeing those private offices, displaying all the accolades they have received. Coders need space, especially if they're juggling multiple screens. Meanwhile, the marketing and sales crew? They're flexible, working from hoteling spots or collaboration tables, just as long as there's a charging point nearby.

Industries and roles are like characters in a play, each with its script. So, the next time you step into the office, remember – everyone's got their groove, and it's what makes the workplace a wild and wonderful ride.

4
RECALIBRATING FOR THE INDUSTRY

Remixes, remixes, remixes — these shapeshifters have taken the world by storm. It is fascinating how a few beats here and a few notes there can transform a popular song into an entirely new and better version of itself! Some versions are tweaked so much that sometimes they lose their soul entirely.

However, some songs retain their essence through eras and trends, even when adapted to every audience's needs. Now, can you ever fathom that the workspace, too, could be remixed according to the needs of their workforce and emerge better than they've ever been? Just imagine a utility corner for all the handsy folks, a reading space for the bookworms, or a chic lounge for a chic organization — all within the premises of an office! Isn't that exciting?

Now, I know one would least expect their workplace to be as reflective of their identity as their favorite corporate-branded t-shirt, but it is possible! Even better, the more adaptable a workplace is to its users' needs, the more it is destined to succeed in its purpose. So, you can set your organization's workplace up for success by reimagining it as a tailorable, resilient, and representative space that aligns with the organization's objectives and meets the diverse needs of your employees. This chapter highlights the importance of designing a workplace adaptable to different industries, work objectives, and employee preferences. It emphasizes the need to move away from a one-size-fits-all approach and instead focus on creating a tailored environment that fosters productivity, collaboration, and innovation. Let's dive in!

Redefining workplaces for the changing world

Even in the 21st century, the words 'corporate' or 'office' ring a very selective bell whenever we hear them: congested cubicles, chilly cabins, dull colors, shared facilities, and a lackluster environment. Most offices still take us back to a couple decades ago with their ancient appearance. In contrast, only a few workspaces have been mindfully crafted with a solid intention to align with modern times and specific organizational goals. Now, while such workspaces might be much better when compared to the stereotypical ones, they still require a complete overhaul and facelift to adapt to a post-COVID-19 world.

These days, everything can be customized to the tiniest details, from shoes and perfume to phones and cars. So, why not workspaces, too? Workspace customization is the latest trend to take the professional world by storm, given the possibilities it creates for an exciting work environment. Organizations can develop workspaces purposely tailored to facilitate interactions that won't be as effective remotely as in-person ones, such as team-building activities, collaborative projects, or even just a game of musical chairs!

Suppose an organization's primary objective is facilitating group projects that encourage collaboration rather than in a dog-eat-dog environment. Shouldn't the office allocate 80% of its space to collaborative rooms? If office space is only required for those who refuse to stare at computer screens all day and would instead stare at real faces, wouldn't it be more practical to provide workspaces near employees' residences? Should organizations encourage those employees who thrive in cubicles to work from home and take introversion too seriously? These are precisely the kinds of questions that must be kept in mind when designing better workspaces.

In 1939, Frank Lloyd Wright presented a revolutionary and innovative concept for the new working environment. His design leapfrogged conventional thinking and set a vision for what could be possible. Through his philosophy of organic architecture, he presented in a variety of ways, including a model of Broadacre City.

With the integration of technology in today's world, I believe technology will embody that famous sofa from the sitcom 'Friends' in future offices. The proper technological assistance will finally convince employees to ditch their pajamas for trousers and work safely at offices before a vaccine comes to the rescue again. Organizations must monitor and manage employee access, entry schedules, cleaning routines, ventilation, social distancing, and AC temperature preferences as employees navigate changing workspaces.

To sustain productivity, teamwork, and learning, and to uphold the corporate culture, any desperate tries to stay complacent and keep working from home must be quashed. In-office videoconferencing can no longer have employees speaking to black screens, cats wreaking havoc, or occasionally high-pitched squabbling in the background. Always-on videoconferencing, seamless integration of in-person and remote tools (virtual whiteboards), and non-simultaneous work models will rapidly transition from visionary concepts to standard practice.

A resilient workspace is thus a dynamic environment consisting of versatile spaces crafted to adjust and develop as needed, efficiently utilizing real estate while promoting increased employee involvement. This leads to a more committed and efficient workforce that works more and plays Candy Crush less, enabling the organization to address shifting business circumstances effectively. For higher engagement from its users, a workspace must be designed for physical, cognitive, and emotional well-being.

A fluid workplace

Since workplaces are constructed with brick and mortar, you might think they are as rigid and unalterable as the mountains in the Himalayas. But the truth is that real estate is anything but static. It is, in fact, as dynamic as a coconut tree swinging in a storm. The workplace doesn't have to be locked up forever if your design responds to people's needs daily. Let's ask why the users or decision-makers must consider flexibility.

A space dedicated to constructing an office could encompass a service building, a workplace, or even a designated section within the office that promotes user customization. This should facilitate various functions, quick adaptability, and straightforward maintenance. Once this is achieved, you establish a space where individuals and teams can tailor their office environment as their needs evolve.

The outcome is a combination of stability and adaptability. Let's think about it this way: a music producer needs his own calm and quiet space, arranged according to his needs (maybe even a smelly sock here and there for decoration purposes) to pump out the best jams. Similarly, individuals and teams require diverse and tailored workspaces and tools for outcomes that reflect their productivity, not how long they twiddled their thumbs.

These needs vary across industries, generations, teams, and individuals as roles become increasingly specialized. Consequently, the range of workstyles in a business necessitates expansion, and entrusting more control to employees becomes an effective workplace strategy.

The advantages are as substantial as a full-course meal. This approach reduces the risk of the unknown, enhances resilience during growth, and minimizes the cost of change, thus hitting three targets with one arrow.

Additionally, it puts a magic spell on employees, pushing them to indulge in more collaborative behaviors and supporting user-driven workstyles, ultimately enhancing individuals' effectiveness. The entrepreneurial spirit that characterizes startup culture represents an appealing objective for larger businesses. They recognize that they possess talent and expertise but encounter challenges in harnessing it with the same swiftness. The freedom to pursue novel ideas and foster innovation becomes accessible when you remove constraining structures and concentrate on the necessary tools for experimentation.

VaynerMedia is a contemporary global creative and media agency that works with some of the most reputable and leading multinational brands, including PepsiCo, P&G, Diageo, and Prudential, among others. Their new Singapore HQ features a 'Maker Space' environment that enables employees to produce social media content conveniently and supports the agency's creative spirit and rapid expansion.

At the heart of the office is 'The Stage,' a vast, multi-functional space that can transform from a working breakout and collaboration area to an event space that hosts inspiring speakers or welcomes all-day workshops. The pantry area and breakout spaces that wrap around 'The Stage' allow people in these spaces to join the event freely and informally.

Designers now devise workplace design solutions on all scales for clients while adopting this approach, ranging from expansive innovation hubs to compact workspaces and adaptable meeting pods. Most businesses do not necessitate an entirely flexible office design to attain their objectives; all that's required is a designated space and a relaxed mindset.

Regardless of the size, the permanent space is continually poised for experimentation.

Workplace design and inclusivity as a tool:

I looked at the new headquarters of Bread Financial, designed by Unispace, featuring many additions that make the space equitable for all associates, including those who are neurodivergent. Bread Financial, a leader in data-driven payment, lending, and saving solutions, was looking to optimize its campus footprint and upgrade its workspaces to increase efficiency and engagement among teams. The design strategy structured by visioning sessions, a company-wide survey, and leadership interviews recommended giving associates autonomy regarding where they work, fostering equity, and encouraging camaraderie amongst the employees. The process recommended that a specific mix of innovation, problem-solving, and community spaces was the right approach to creating the associate experience they were looking for.

My takeaway was the engagement that the designers had with the company, which started with a visioning session with their executives to understand their way ahead, where they want to steer the company over the course of the next few years, and how their workplace design can help meet that vision.

Apprehending the importance of the associates' input, to create a more holistic understanding of Bread Financial, the design team also conducted a company-wide workplace survey and interviewed key leaders throughout the organization. The planning resulted in the decision to create three themes for the new office – autonomy, equity, and camaraderie – which required the space to be designed in a way that would support these themes.

Alignment for the win

Moving beyond the one-size-fits-all approach to workplace designs, a competent designer must first grasp the diverse dynamics of an organization's structure before embarking on the planning process. They should understand how varying management styles and the age demographics of employees can significantly influence workplace design.

For instance, a hierarchical healthcare or legal organization may require a different design approach than a flat tech firm. Similarly, the workplace requirements of a youthful startup may markedly differ from those of a company with a predominantly older workforce.

Influential designers possess a range of tools to assess the current state of an organization. They should use quantitative methods such as surveys and space utilization data, as well as qualitative methods like interviews and observations, to comprehensively understand the strengths and weaknesses of the workplace, with specific consideration for the industry.

Workstyle plays a pivotal role. For instance, tech companies often promote cross-functional collaborations, necessitating spaces designed to foster such interactions. In contrast, oil and gas companies might require more specialized rooms to cater to their distinct operational needs.

As the world of work evolves, workplace design must adapt and be customized, taking into account emerging trends like hybrid working, where employees divide their time between the office and remote work.

Designers should be prepared with innovative ideas to create flexible and adaptable spaces to accommodate these new work trends. Workplace design is not a one-size-fits-all proposition; the most effective approach is to approach each project and industry with a clear, specific set of criteria considering each client's unique needs and characteristics. The uniqueness of each organization should be reflected in its workplace design.

Now, let's delve deeper into how work styles vary by industry. Shortly after the pandemic, Unispace surveyed their clients on this topic. In finance, legal, accounting, mining, natural resources, utilities, construction, the public sector, and publishing, the average balance shifts to Problem-solving at 45%, Community at 30%, and innovation. Meanwhile, for businesses in pharmaceuticals, biotech, technology, data, logistics, fashion, beauty, and manufacturing, the balance shifts to Innovation at 50%, problem-solving at 25%, and the community at 25%. In consulting, media, the arts, property, creative fields, and insurance, work is divided as follows: Community 45%, Innovation 30%, Problem-solving 25%.

Individuals require a highly tailored workspace to be content, comfortable, and productive. This will impact the types of spaces they use (and when), their physical environment, furnishings, equipment, amenities, sensory experiences, and much more.

Zone and space design will be of utmost importance. Individual offices, as are rows of closely packed desks, are a thing of the past. The future lies in flexible, organic, shared spaces where people can engage in effective teamwork, as individual work is increasingly likely to be completed at home.

In such zones, people should be emotionally and physically stimulated to perform at their best. They can benefit from curated experiences that optimize their productivity.

Benefits of a flexible and responsive workspace

The evolving nature of business, especially in uncertain times, necessitates a re-evaluation of traditional approaches to office space. The need for flexibility in workspace utilization has become increasingly apparent as businesses experience fluctuations in space requirements due to factors such as project-based team onboarding, varying types of meetings, and the need for versatile spaces accommodating diverse functions.

In the wake of the pandemic-induced disruptions, the conventional model of assigning a fixed number of seats and meeting rooms may no longer be effective. One could respond to this challenge by working closely with designers to ensure that flexibility is a fundamental element of the design process. The trend among large enterprises is a growing reliance on coworking facilities, whether for a portion of their space or the entire area, on a temporary or semi-permanent basis. This strategic use of coworking spaces allows organizations to supplement their existing infrastructure, providing the crucial flexibility required in today's dynamic business environment.

The evolving demand for office spaces after the pandemic

Surveys indicate that flexibility has emerged as a central theme in the evolving demand for office spaces in all industry types. In the past, we tied this with start-ups and smaller tech firms; now, co-working spaces are experiencing a surge in popularity as businesses seek agile solutions.

These spaces empower companies to scale their office footprint based on current needs, offering cost-effective options and the agility to respond to changing work patterns. Notably, short-term lease agreements are gaining favor, reflecting a desire for adaptable solutions in the dynamic landscape of modern business. When it comes to furnishing new office spaces, we are seeing a pronounced emphasis on adaptability, with workspaces designed to encourage innovation and team collaboration in a hybrid environment.

In essence, the office is evolving into a holistic hub that supports productivity and prioritizes the physical and mental well- being of our employees. As we navigate this transformative period, Unispace remains at the forefront, actively shaping the future of workspaces to meet the dynamic needs of the modern business landscape.

The common thread among these diverse applications is the core attribute of flexibility.

In this context, flexibility refers to expanding or contracting space at short notice without being tied down by lengthy leases. This flexibility extends to the adaptability of space usage, allowing businesses to configure the space to suit specific needs, even on short notice and often within minutes. This dynamic approach to space utilization aligns with the agile and adaptive nature of modern business requirements.

Achieving space-saving and cost-saving flexibility necessitates a comprehensive understanding of how the current footprint is utilized and what activities should occur within that space.

Discussions about workplace design with leaders revolve around an organization's objectives and principles—what it aims to accomplish and the strategies it employs to do so. These messages are conveyed through various communication channels, both subtle and overt. When effectively executed, they significantly enhance employee engagement, loyalty, and innovation. Conversely, inadequate communication, characterized by inconsistency, infrequency, or ambiguity, hampers the organization's ability to uphold its brand identity and deliver on its promises.

Reflecting on a design workshop with TiVo's leadership in Bangalore, it was clear that beyond reflecting the brand and its values their unique requirements for open office workstations were pivotal. Being a leader in entertainment technology and audience insights, they needed workstations tailored to accommodate multiple set-top boxes and various TX screens essential for their engineers. In-depth discussions with user representatives and leaders provided deep insights into their work processes. This led to the creation of not just functional workstations but also "idea zones"—spaces designed to promote creative thinking, innovation, and concept development. These spaces feature clustered seating for 360- degree views and writable surfaces for brainstorming, ensuring design continuity and transparency throughout the reception and open office areas.

This case study highlights how TiVo's innovative approach to workspace design meets the evolving specific needs and function of its employees, particularly the younger generation, and fosters a productive and dynamic working environment, a typical tech office design wouldn't have suited them at all.

People are paramount to the success of an organization and the execution of its workplace strategy. However, they can also be central to organizational challenges. As Henry Ford famously remarked, "Coming together is a beginning. Keeping together is progress. Working together is success." Effective workplace design plays a crucial role in enabling companies to achieve this success by fostering employee engagement. By creating a workspace conducive to collaboration and interaction, organizations can empower their employees to work together seamlessly towards common goals. A Visioning Session with stakeholders and leadership is a great place to unearth project priorities and values that will serve as a consistent thread throughout the duration of the work. Visioning Sessions are a unique, interactive opportunity to bring together stakeholders to build consensus around big ideas before the design process even begins.

Leaders are responsible for modeling inclusive behaviors and prioritizing diversity, equity, and inclusivity. Leaders must walk the talk and, in doing so, can better meet the needs of their people, customers, and communities. In every conversation with clients before kick-starting a workplace design, I have found a common thread: People are the most critical factor in the success of an organization and the implementation of its workplace strategy. Likewise, the conversations are structured around these key questions to help create spaces that reflect and promote workplace strategies.

Some of these include:
- What are the organization's goals and values?
- What can companies do to energize and engage the workforce?
- How can the workplace impact productivity?
- How can design innovations help improve quality of life and work?
- What does success look like?

Embracing a people-centered and strategic approach to design is a powerful way to face the constant change and challenges at work, optimize results, and reward efforts with success, satisfaction, and joy.

As we continue our exploration of workplace dynamics, the next chapter will dive into the need for a brand-new, wonderful kid on the workplace-design block—hyper-flexibility. Read on to find out more about it!

5
HYPER FLEXIBILITY
& NEW WAYS OF WORKING

Imagine being surrounded by sun, sand, and sea on a picturesque island, sipping your favorite drink and creating a presentation. The next day, you're in the scenic hills of Manali, curled up in a blanket and submitting the day's work report to your supervisor. "But wait, don't people normally work from an office and not a hotel room halfway around the world?" Well, thanks to the aftereffects of the pandemic, not anymore! Welcome to an era of hyper flexibility, where you only need a laptop and an internet connection to complete all your professional tasks without being confined to a stereotypical office space! Workplaces are becoming increasingly adaptive to hyper flexibility and the novel working methods embraced by the millennial and Gen Z generations.

This chapter explores the concept of hyper-flexibility in the workplace and highlights the importance of designing spaces that accommodate new ways of working. It aims to provide insights into strategies for creating an environment that supports dynamic work practices, enhances collaboration, and promotes employee well-being.

What exactly is hyper flexibility?

In the pre-pandemic era, the concept of a workplace would only bring up images of a cubicle or a drab office, and it was absolutely necessary for employees to be physically present for a significant portion of their work hours. The landscape has undergone a seismic shift, and now work is not confined to a specific location—it can unfold at the office, in the comfort of one's home, virtually anywhere in between. With the advent of Work-From-Home culture post-pandemic, employees soon realized that the H in WFH could stand for Hotel, Hawaii, or even the Himalayas! The latest H to take the professional realm by storm worldwide is Hyper flexibility, and you must have already formed an idea of what it is all about.

Unlike the traditional work setup where employers dictate the terms and conditions, hyper-flexibility empowers modern professionals to craft their jobs around their lifestyles. In this brave new world, the employees hold the reins, steering the direction of their professional journey. They are no longer passive recipients of workplace norms; instead, they actively participate in defining what work means to them and how it should seamlessly blend with their lives. The paradigm has flipped; it is no longer a case of fitting life into the contours of work, but rather, tailoring work to integrate into the fabric of one's life seamlessly. This paradigm shift acknowledges employees' diverse needs and preferences and recognizes that productivity is not bound to a specific physical location. The WFH culture, once a temporary response to a crisis, has evolved into a dynamic force reshaping the very foundations of the professional landscape. When people have control over when, where, and how they work, they are more likely to feel empowered and engaged in their roles, resulting in higher job satisfaction and motivation.

Providing employees with the flexibility they desire and require has become increasingly important to a thriving workplace and increased trust within the workforce. In 2022, a survey by leading tech organization Atlassian found that out of the 1710 knowledge workers surveyed across the USA and Australia, 36% who didn't receive any flexibility in choosing their location of work experienced symptoms of severe burnout and exhaustion, compared to 14% of surveyees who were allowed some flexibility. Also, while 47% of those employees who didn't receive any flexibility benefits still managed to hold on to a positive outlook towards work, a whopping 83% of those receiving some flexibility had an optimistic view of their work environment.

Here are a few defining factors of the hyper flexibility model for you to understand the concept better:

For starters, hyper-flexibility extends beyond typical working hours. It allows employees to tailor their work hours to their most productive times and personal preferences. This adaptability recognizes that various people have varying energy levels and creative inclinations throughout the day, allowing them to optimize their jobs for peak performance. Furthermore, rather than adhering to a fixed schedule, hyper flexibility adopts a task-based work structure in which the number of tasks an employee has in a given workday takes precedence over the period during which an employee signs in for work. The emphasis moves to outcomes and results, creating a results-driven workplace culture. Employers evaluate employees based on their job quality, capacity to meet deadlines, and achievement of daily goals rather than micromanaging their day-to-day operations. On these same lines, hyper flexibility frequently entails implementing hybrid work models that combine remote work and in-office collaboration, promoting a balance between solo work and collaborative team efforts. Many firms are already catching up with the trend, providing two of every five working days for WFH and the other days for in-office work.

Employees are free to choose their work environment, one of the most significant benefits of hyper-flexibility. Someone may perform well in a cubicle, while another may flourish working in nature. Employees can avail themselves of the setting that best supports their productivity and well-being, whether they work from home, in a co- working space, in a coffee shop, or while traveling. Technology plays a crucial role in providing hyper-flexibility. Cloud-based collaboration tools, videoconferencing, project management platforms, and communication apps enable employees to stay connected and interact smoothly, regardless of their physical location. Finally, the days of working 12 hours a day and barely having time for yourself are over. Hyper flexibility facilitates a comprehensive approach to work-life balance and integration. Employees can effortlessly balance personal and professional commitments without the constraints of a traditional office setting.

These are all the ways hyperflexibility makes the professional world a better place for all of us to work!

Millennial and GenZ Prayers Answered!

How vital is hyper flexibility in meeting the needs of millennial and Gen Z employees?

Although millennials and GenZ may have different ideas about work processes and culture, they want the same things regarding benefits at the workplace. Both generations have been found to suffer from heightened anxiety and a sense of suffocation from strict rules and deadlines than the older generations. That is why millennials and GenZs unitedly prioritize work-life balance and flexible work culture.

The Millennials laid the foundations for better flexibility and well-being at work, but the GenZs are turning the exception into the norm. Once upon a time, GenX was taken aback when millennials started speaking up for their rights at work. It is a time-tested tradition—the younger/newer generations always seem more advanced than the last.

That is why Millennials and GenZs are making full use of the resources and benefits available to them, thanks to the revolution in work culture in just the past few years.

In 2021, a study from IWG showed that 84% of 18- to 24-year-olds would rather work in organizations that encourage flexible working practices than receive a 10% hike in their salary. This indicates that the younger generation has begun to place more value on having a say in their work schedules and travel habits. This is especially true for modern professionals who know what they want and aren't afraid to ask for it. When I speak to HR professionals about current hiring trends, they always tell me that the number one preference that candidates ask for is hybrid working, a combination of Work From Home and Work From Office.

With the proliferation of remote work and flexible arrangements, organizations can attract and give opportunities to skilled professionals from diverse backgrounds and geographical locations, enriching the talent pool with various perspectives and experiences. This not only fosters a more innovative and creative work environment but also aligns with the goals of the younger generations. Moreover, hyper-flexibility is important for employee retention among millennials and GenZ. These generations place a high value on their well-being and work-life balance. Mental health support, fitness initiatives, and other well-being resources contribute to a supportive and nurturing workplace culture, aligning with the values of professionals worldwide. Organizations prioritizing a flexible work environment are more likely to retain talent, leading to the eventual creation of a team of dedicated professionals who are also immensely talented and valuable. The adaptability of hyper flexibility to personal circumstances is especially important for employees experiencing rapid changes in their lives. Whether starting families or pursuing higher studies, the flexibility to adjust work schedules and locations allows individuals to balance personal and professional commitments without a hitch.

On these lines, some professionals have taken the concept of hyper flexibility one notch higher. These entrepreneurs, founders, and freelancers who have been branded 'digital nomads' are now estimated to be 35 million strong worldwide. Digital nomads are "people who embrace a location-independent, technology-enabled lifestyle that allows them to travel and work anywhere in the interconnected world. They utilize technology to work remotely and move frequently from one place to another while still fulfilling their professional commitments. This lifestyle allows people to live and work anywhere they wish, freeing them from the confines of a set place. To support their dynamic lifestyle, digital nomads usually rely on various skills such as programming, writing, design, and digital marketing. A recent report revealed that 61% of this community is in their 20s or 30s.

Here are some interesting facts
1. 40 million people in the world right now are digital nomads.
2. 62% of digital nomads identify as male.
3. 46% of digital nomads are American.
4. 91% of digital nomads report having a higher education.

5. 62% of digital nomads hold traditional full-time positions.
6. 70% of digital nomads work 40 hours or less per week.
7. 60% of digital nomads work from a home office.
8. 77% of digital nomads report being early adopters of technology.
9. 82% of digital nomads report feeling very satisfied with their income.

(Source: Digital Nomad Statistics You Should Know 2024; pumble.com)

The workplaces of tomorrow must be designed to support employees who choose to work more dynamically. To facilitate effective teamwork and collaboration, facilities should be made available at all times of day, including early in the morning and late in the evening, as well as throughout the day for refreshments and restroom breaks. There should also be enough space during peak hours to accommodate the workforce. Growing up in an era of fast technological and business model change, millennials and Generation Zs have long been known for their adaptability and ability to change course in the workplace when necessary. It is no longer merely about accommodating an individual's needs; it extends to changing work hours, practices, and schedules to deliver optimal performance and support employee well-being.

Thus, hyper flexibility is a transformative force that goes beyond meeting the needs of millennials, GenZs, and even digital nomads; it reshapes the fabric of work culture, accommodating diverse lifestyles, preferences, and even ages. As the younger generations continue to drive the change, the professional landscape evolves into a space where autonomy, well-being, and innovative thinking are at the forefront, creating a future of work that is as dynamic as the individuals shaping it.

Strategies for Designing Flexible Workspaces

Future workplaces must also be built to accommodate workers who choose a more dynamic work environment. To enable teams to work cooperatively and effectively, for instance, it is essential to ensure that buildings are accessible early in the morning and late at night, refreshments and restrooms are available all day, and enough room for the workforce during peak working hours. Because they experienced fast changes in business structures and technology as youngsters, Gen Z and millennials are known for their adaptability and capacity to shift course in the workplace when necessary. The concept of flexible workspaces is no longer only about meeting an individual's demands; it also includes changing work hours, procedures, and schedules to achieve optimal performance while supporting employee well-being. That being stated, workplace design would actively contribute to people attaining hyper-flexibility.

Here are some strategies:

1. **Choice seating and Quiet areas:** Choice seating, also known as flexible seating, is a workplace design concept that moves away from assigned desks and cubicles. Instead, employees are offered a variety of work settings to choose from throughout the day. This could include quiet zones for focused work, open, collaborative spaces for brainstorming sessions, standing desks for those who prefer to work on their feet, or even comfy lounge areas for taking a break. The idea behind choice seating is to empower employees to work in a way that best suits them and their tasks.

2. **Variation of spaces across the floor plate:** Ensuring the availability of a wide array of spaces would give freedom to the employees, from collaboration areas and work pods to standing desks, treadmill desks, or even designated walking paths can cater to the employees who prefer working on their feet or taking short activity breaks.

3. **Access to power and technology:** The absolute need of the hour, ideally, every ergonomic seat where employees are expected to sit should have a provision to draw power and also have flexible screens or AV to ensure that space is utilized for meetings or n-call interactions with remote teams or other entities.

4. **Shared resources:** These could be any equipment, facilities, or amenities that are used by multiple employees. These resources can be physical or digital, and their effective management is crucial for a smooth-functioning, effective, and efficient workplace.

A Success Story

I have heard first-hand experiences from friends who gladly adapted to the new ways of working, one of them being a young engineer with a leading tech firm in Bangalore. The advancement of hybrid work schedules has proven to be a game-changer for her, representing a particular group of people known as the "sandwich generation." These are middle-aged adults - often between their 40s and 50s - caught between raising their children and caring for aging parents. Before the rise of hybrid work models, she and similar individuals often felt like they were in a tug-of-war, being pulled in multiple directions simultaneously. But now, the scales have shifted dramatically.

The adaptability of hybrid work has made this previously insurmountable juggling act more bearable, even enjoyable. It's as if they've been given a magic wand that transforms a high-risk balancing act into a well-choreographed ballet. Let's call the protagonist of our example Aisha. Aisha is in the midst of her workday. She would be in her office in a traditional job environment, away from her aging mother and children. Working remotely now allows her to attend a virtual meeting, then quickly switch gears to assist her child with schoolwork and later prepare her mother for a doctor's appointment without leaving the house.

This seamless merging of professional and personal lives is now a reality owing to hybrid work. The days of Aisha hurrying through Bangalore's never-ending traffic, frantically checking the clock as she rushes from the office to the hospital or home, are over. Now, Aisha can fulfill her role as a caring daughter and mother, all while continuing to excel in her career.

Moreover, this shift doesn't just benefit Aisha. It's positively impacting her entire family. Her elderly mother enjoys more time with her family, her children get more attention and supervision, and Aisha feels less worried and more satisfied. This new employment model has allowed her the freedom to manage her time better and the gratification of knowing she is available to her loved ones.

In this regard, the rise of remote and hybrid work models is more than a trend; it is a societal movement that empowers the "sandwich generation" and changes the dynamics of family care. It's a radical change that profoundly impacts families, businesses, and communities nationwide.

What About the Flipside?

Embracing the world of hyper-flexible work conditions is like negotiating a treacherous terrain where new ideas collide with old obstacles. Organizations are entering an exciting period where the old office boundaries are blurring, and the possibilities seem infinite as they embrace the freeing concept of flexible scheduling, task-based frameworks, and hybrid work models. However, every venture into uncharted territory has its shadows, casting concerns that demand attention.

Imagine a workplace where employees love the flexibility to work anywhere they choose, so they travel the world and set up shop at co-working locations. Yet, amid the allure of jet-setting and limitless flexibility, an unforeseen challenge lurks – the risk of losing touch with our human side. Loneliness can quietly seep in, missing the water cooler banter, the coffee breaks, and the camaraderie of impromptu team lunches. In this section, we will delve into the flipside of hyper-flexibility, unraveling the complexities that arise from the blurring of work-life boundaries, communication hurdles, and the evolving nature of workspace design.

Forgetting to socialize:

In a hyper-flexible work environment, employees have the freedom to choose when and where they work. While this can lead to increased productivity and work-life balance, it can also result in a lack of regular social interactions. Without a structured environment that naturally fosters social connections - such as an office with shared spaces—employees might prioritize work over socializing. The absence of casual, in-person interactions can lead to feelings of isolation, reduce team bonding, and diminish the overall sense of community within the organization.

Blurred lines between work and personal life:

Hyper-flexibility often means that work can extend beyond the traditional 9-to-5 schedule. Employees may work at odd hours or mix work with personal activities throughout the day. While this can be beneficial for managing personal responsibilities, it can also blur the boundaries between work and personal life. Employees might find themselves constantly thinking about work or feeling compelled to be "on" at all times, even during personal time. This lack of clear separation can lead to stress, burnout, and difficulty in truly disconnecting from work.

Communication and culture-building challenges:

With employees working at different times and from various locations, coordinating communication becomes more complex. Asynchronous communication, while convenient, can lead to delays in responses, misunderstandings, and a lack of immediate feedback. Moreover, the informal ways in which company culture is usually built—through shared experiences, spontaneous interactions, and collective rituals—are harder to maintain in a hyper-flexible workstyle. The diverse working hours and locations can make it challenging to create a unified, cohesive culture, potentially leading to a sense of disconnection among employees.

Security:
The more flexible and dispersed the workforce, the greater the challenge in maintaining robust security. Employees working from different locations and using various devices and networks increase the risk of security vulnerabilities. Home networks and public Wi-Fi are generally less secure than corporate networks, making it easier for cyber threats to exploit weaknesses. Additionally, with the freedom to use personal devices, there may be inconsistencies in security measures, such as software updates, encryption, and secure access protocols. This can lead to increased risks of data breaches, unauthorized access, and other security issues.

When I think of flexibility, one of the workplace design projects that comes to mind is Bottomline's office. Amidst the challenges of the pandemic and a sudden and swift shift to remote work, our goal was clear: to design a space that would draw people back into the office and foster connections among teams, old and new. Bottomline wanted more than just a workplace – they wanted a home away from home, a place their staff would be proud to call their own.

Bottomline's reputation for simplifying complex payments made it clear that their workspace needed to be anything but ordinary. With a focus on innovative design and a nod to the company's forward-thinking ethos, we set out to create a space that would not only inspire creativity but also serve as a hub for collaboration and community-building. From vibrant meeting spaces to cozy nooks designed for brainstorming sessions, every inch of the workspace was crafted with Bottomline's vision in mind.

The neighborhood model, widely used for designing office spaces, is outdated and no longer functional. It is gradually being replaced by zoning spaces that cater to different needs. These spaces are categorized into "me," "we," and "us" spaces. The "me" spaces consist of individual, focused workspaces such as pods, phone booths, and small private rooms. "We" spaces include a range of areas for small group collaboration, such as conference rooms and meeting spaces. "Us" spaces include lounges, cafes, and other casual areas with varied seating options, providing an alternative environment for individual work or small group meetings while facilitating connections with colleagues. Offering this variety helps replicate and enhance the flexibility and control employees experience while working from home.

The future workplace hinges on the organization and zoning of spaces. In a hybrid work scenario, reverting to a neighborhood model can lead to wasted space. Instead of trying to impress employees with random perks like cooking classes and masala chai carts, employers should focus on making the office a more effective environment for work than home. Creating an environment that truly boosts productivity, both for individuals and groups, is crucial. This begins with ensuring a reliable and robust internet and power connection. It's essential to provide seamless and stable internet while enabling easier access to power sockets across all seating arrangements in the office to limit the need for employees to search for better connectivity spots, positively impacting their ability to connect well and use resources and tools effectively.

Hyper-flexibility does not work for everyone. People work differently, and when it comes to office design, you may discover that some people flourish in an open style where everyone can communicate quickly, while others prefer privacy. A well-functioning hyper-flexible workspace should be considered, creating space/opportunity for independent working. So, customization is essential, and the right workplace design can help employers and employees find the right balance of space, the right balance of collaboration spaces vs focused spaces vs community spaces.

This is where Bottomline made a change in the system. They understood that to truly elevate their workspace, they needed to break free from the traditional engineering desk-centric setup. With a majority of their staff being engineers, it was crucial to carve out ample space for focused work while also fostering collaboration and solution-driven interactions.

Enter a new era of workspace design. They transformed the landscape, creating clusters of ergonomic workstations tailored for deep focus. They challenged the status quo, introducing drop-in team tables and cozy acoustic booths for impromptu brainstorms and quick chats.

Surrounding these hubs of productivity was an array of meeting rooms, flexible, collaborative spaces, and a buzzing innovation center – the heart of it all.

And let's talk aesthetics. Color played a starring role, injecting life into collaborative areas, fostering focus in work zones, and energizing community spaces. Plus, they didn't forget to weave in local Bangalore culture, infusing the space with carefully curated environmental graphics and artwork.

But perhaps the most groundbreaking move? Bottomline's shift to an agile work policy, where seating became unassigned, promoting fluidity and collaboration like never before. Through meticulous planning and modeling, we ensured Bottomline's workspace was not just future-proofed but ready to adapt to whatever the future might bring.

As the younger generation's work expectations shift toward employee experience, the expectation towards workplace design has also shifted. Design is no longer a siloed form of work. One must design holistic outcomes for emotion, experience, transformation, and possibilities.

Now that we have explored the realm of hyper-flexibility, we can move on to discussing the prioritization of employee well-being in the workplace, something that is very close to the Gen-Z heart.

6
MOVE TO PRACTICAL WELLNESS:
PRIORITIZING EMPLOYEE WELL-BEING IN THE WORKPLACE

Covid has been a pain to the world, and post the virus era, coworking became the new normal. Although we slowly marched away from the virus, we still carry emotional baggage from the past, don't we? During the pandemic, it was not just the virus that took people's lives; people suffered from agitated depressive disorders, pushing them to the precipice of succumbing to negative thoughts. Therefore, coworking spaces now have to customize everything in a way that caters to everyone.

The truth is the success of every organization is in the hands of its employees. A happy employee can bring abundance to the company in ways that they cannot imagine.

Research and studies have increasingly portrayed how a healthy and content workforce can significantly contribute to a company's success in numerous ways. Let's look at some key factors that come to mind.

Enhanced Employee Engagement:

If you provide a safe working environment for your employees, the chances of them engaging positively with the organization are likely very high. Apart from being highly competitive, the company needs to give precedence to the welfare of the employees, abiding by the "Employee Value Proposition' framework. This framework helps you become an appealing employer. The moment your team realizes you value their esteemed presence and contribute so much to their welfare, they will willingly be involved in productive tasks. Engaged staff members exhibit greater productivity, provide considerate and individualized customer experiences, demonstrate dedication to exploration and enhancement, experience heightened job contentment, and have a reduced inclination to depart from the company, resulting in escalated retention statistics.

Now, how do we ensure engagement in workplace design? If you are even in an early conversation about building a new workplace for your employees, engaging them in the design and creation of their workspace can significantly enhance motivation, productivity, and overall job satisfaction. This approach not only improves the workplace but also fosters a sense of belonging and commitment among employees, leading to a more positive and productive work environment.

Leadership's role in the workplace design process is crucial. Forming design committees that include employees from various departments and levels within the company ensures diverse perspectives are considered. These committees can brainstorm, discuss, and propose design ideas collaboratively. Organizing workshops and brainstorming sessions further involves employees in the design process. Pilot programs and prototyping are also beneficial; developing pilot workspaces or zones based on employee feedback allows testing and refinement before final implementation. Prototyping gives employees a chance to experience and provide feedback on potential designs.

In my recent experience, I can't think of any workplace project where someone from leadership alone makes all decisions, or it's a conversation limited to the facilities group! Instead, in most of the projects, I have had wonderful experiences engaging with professionals from different backgrounds who were passionately involved in workplace design. This indeed explains that, as an industry, we have progressed a lot, but as always, there is room for growth to get more diverse voices to the table in these processes.

Spaces that foster a supportive work environment:

Crafting a workplace layout that speaks to employee happiness and well-being is pivotal. Imagine an office where open spaces reign supreme, breathing life into the environment. These airy expanses not only liberate but also create a cozy, relaxed atmosphere, setting the stage for elevated job satisfaction and enhanced company performance.

Picture this: employees empowered with the autonomy to shape their workspaces. From serene corners for focused work to dynamic, collaborative hubs and cozy relaxation nooks, the possibilities are endless. By putting the reins in their hands, you're fueling their comfort and fulfillment like never before.

But wait, there's more! Strategic design sparks spontaneous dialogues among colleagues, sparking creativity and camaraderie. Picture bustling communal areas, shared tables, and inviting breakout spots—all designed to foster teamwork and ignite innovation. With every interaction, your workforce becomes more productive, more engaged, and happier than ever before.

Designing an environment that creates an engaging and enjoyable experience:

Crafting an environment that truly captivates and delights individuals is paramount in today's workplace landscape. As we've explored in previous discussions on workplace experience, it's evident that the heart of every business outcome lies with its employees. To propel productivity, efficiency, talent retention, innovation, and growth, a fresh perspective is essential—one that seamlessly integrates technology, operations, culture, and employee experience. Enter WX, or "Workplace Experience," the brainchild of today's pioneering workplace design leaders.

WX represents a paradigm shift, embracing a holistic approach that prioritizes cost efficiency, productivity, and growth. It's not just about offering the latest tech gadgets; it's about nurturing human experiences and digital interfaces. From streamlining the transition between office and remote work to optimizing job performance through cutting-edge technologies, WX leaves no stone unturned in enhancing the overall workplace experience.

In essence, WX embodies a fusion of technology, operations, culture, and employee experience, ushering in a new era where the workplace becomes a dynamic hub of innovation, collaboration, and personal fulfillment. By placing emphasis on both the physical environment and digital tools, WX paves the way for a seamless, empowering journey for every individual within the organization.

Transparency:

Embracing openness isn't just a trend—it's a cornerstone of fostering employee well-being. While transparency is often championed in customer interactions, its importance within the company cannot be overstated. When employees have access to relevant information, understand company protocols, and see how their efforts contribute to organizational goals, trust blossoms, and a sense of belonging flourishes.

Gone are the days of closed-off cubicles; open office layouts now reign supreme. But it doesn't stop there. Cultivate an environment where the door is always open—metaphorically, of course. Encourage a culture where employees feel empowered to voice their concerns, share their ideas, and offer suggestions without hesitation. The days of secluded corner offices for managers are a thing of the past. In today's workplace, inclusivity and collaboration take center stage.

When employees feel heard and valued, they become active participants in wellness initiatives and champions of the organization's success. By fostering an atmosphere of openness and accessibility, companies not only enhance employee well-being but also cultivate a culture of innovation, engagement, and mutual respect.

Now, let's get back to the physical aspect of wellness and how a thoughtfully designed office could promote wellness. The economic case for investment in wellbeing is clear. While initially, organizations are likely to incur additional costs, the business case for investment is strong. According to a recent Harvard Business Review case study, Johnson & Johnson's leaders estimated that their wellness programs had saved the company millions in healthcare costs over the past decade. As we dive deep into further chapters, younger generations like Gen Z are hyper-conscious about health and activity.

Incorporating well-being concepts into workplace design:

Creating a workplace that truly prioritizes the well-being of its occupants requires a holistic approach that encompasses both physical and psychological health. It's not just about safeguarding our bodies; it's about nurturing minds and spirits, too. Here are some ideas to achieve this:

- **Design for Mental Health:** Stress is a pervasive issue in modern workplaces, stemming from factors like lack of control, enclosed spaces, poor lighting, and interruptions. Stress-reducing design principles can mitigate these issues. Introducing natural materials, maximizing external views, and flooding spaces with sunlight can alleviate stress, enhance memory, and promote positive emotions. Incorporating tactile elements like wood and water can further engage employees with their surroundings, fostering a sense of calm and connection.

- **Spaces for Breaks and Movement:** Encouraging movement and providing dedicated areas for breaks are vital for boosting both physical and mental well-being. Spaces designed to facilitate clean air circulation promote health and comfort while fostering a sense of community and collaboration. Offering amenities like gyms, on-demand yoga sessions, gaming areas, and quiet zones provides employees with opportunities to unwind, reflect, and recharge. These amenities not only combat work fatigue but also promote productivity and foster positive mindsets.

Companies like Novo Nordisk exemplify this commitment to well-being through thoughtful workplace design. Their comfortable breakrooms and game rooms offer employees much-needed mental breaks, helping them avoid burnout. By incorporating biophilic elements and collaborative zones, Novo Nordisk creates environments that promote relaxation, connection, and vitality. Additionally, innovative features like custom rock-climbing walls inspire employees to embrace healthy, active lifestyles continuously.

By embracing these principles and investing in the well-being of their workforce, organizations not only attract top talent but also ensure their continued success and productivity. After all, employees are the lifeblood of any business, and prioritizing their well-being is essential for long-term growth and prosperity.

A yoga/multipurpose room design

Ergonomic furniture and layout:

Fostering a company culture that prioritizes employee well-being involves a range of strategies aimed at promoting healthy habits and enhancing overall wellness. From encouraging breaks in natural surroundings to implementing flexible work schedules, every detail counts. One such crucial detail is ergonomic furniture—a seemingly small aspect of workplace design that plays a significant role in supporting staff wellness.

In today's office environments, where many employees spend prolonged hours in front of computer screens, the selection of workspace furniture is more critical than ever. Uncomfortable chairs, improper desk setups, and inadequate natural light can gradually take a toll on physical health and contribute to stress over time. This is where ergonomic design shines.

Ergonomic furniture is designed with the human body in mind, aiming to promote comfort, support, and movement throughout the workday. By incorporating ergonomic elements into the office environment, organizations can significantly impact both mental and physical well-being. Take standing desks, for example—they not only reduce the risk of back pain but also improve circulation and foster alertness, promoting a healthier and more dynamic work experience.

With a plethora of ergonomic office furniture options available, ranging from standing desks to ergonomic chairs, organizations can tailor their workspace to suit a variety of interior design styles while prioritizing employee health and wellness. By actively integrating into the workday and providing ergonomic solutions, companies can mitigate the health risks associated with sedentary behavior and create a workspace that supports employee well-being on all fronts.

Some of the best options for a healthy workplace include Adjustable standing desks/height adjustable workstations, ergonomic chairs with lumbar support, adjustable keyboard trays, monitor stands to reduce eye strain, and footrests to reduce pressure on the feet. Selecting ergonomic office furniture necessitates careful consideration of the unique requirements of your employees and the nature of their work.

There's no universal solution that fits all scenarios, so I am highlighting the importance of potentially engaging a workplace wellness design consultant for specialized guidance in these matters. Their expertise can offer tailored advice aligned with your employees' diverse needs and job roles, ensuring a more suitable and beneficial ergonomic setup.

Something worth mentioning here is a recent study that highlights that standing desks may not be as beneficial for health as once thought. While they reduce sedentary time, prolonged standing can cause discomfort and potential musculoskeletal issues. The research suggests a more balanced approach to workplace ergonomics, incorporating both sitting and standing periods.

Ensuring all basic Comforts

Indoor Air Quality:
Indoor Air Quality (IAQ) plays a vital role in shaping a healthy office, optimizing productivity and cognitive function while indirectly reducing absenteeism. It refers to the cleanliness and safety of the air within a building, encompassing a variety of potentially harmful pollutants, VOCs, dust particles, and so on. By reducing the risk of allergies and respiratory problems, workers are assured of a healthier office environment in which to work daily. Investing in IAQ creates an appealing, healthy workspace, cultivates employee well-being, and boosts productivity.

Acoustic Comfort:
Acoustic comfort pertains to the quality of sound within indoor settings and its influence on individuals working in those spaces. In the pursuit of designing a workspace that prioritizes wellness, ensuring a high level of both perceived and actual acoustic comfort holds particular significance for mental health. Effective sound management can profoundly improve workplace wellness by mitigating stress caused by excessive noise in office environments. Studies indicate that poorly managed noise levels in offices negatively affect the focus, resulting in headaches, distractions, and low-level stress that hinder rather than enhance productivity. Establishing a serene workspace with an optimal level of ambient background sound (emphasizing "sound" over "noise") allows employers to confidently foster employee health in their everyday work environment. There are some key strategies you can adapt during the design to ensure there is acoustic comfort for the users, such as the use of the right materials to avoid reverberations, the Use of double glazing for partitions to avoid noise transfers, the usage of acoustic panels as part of the finishes, Isolating HVAC and other noise-producing equipment from work areas, etc. There are also advanced technologies like sound masking and biophilic soundscaping, one of which could add additional comfort.

Thermal Comfort:

Perhaps this is one of the most debated subjects in conversations between facility managers and employees simply because this is something extremely personal to each individual. Achieving thermal comfort is essential for promoting overall well-being in the workplace. When employers are uncomfortable due to a deviation from their optimal thermal environment, they become disengaged with their work, focusing too much on staying warm or cooling off, resulting in lower satisfaction and productivity. This also is very challenging to achieve as two people sitting close by can have completely different preferences. The key would be to get an optimum temperature across the floor spaces while building as much flexibility as possible and using VAVs and thermostats for zone-based controls.

Other areas which need a careful look at are:
- **Placement of Inlet and Return Air Grills:** Have you ever noticed those inconspicuous grills in your office ceiling? They play a vital role in maintaining a comfortable and healthy indoor environment. Proper placement of these grills ensures efficient circulation of fresh air while effectively removing stale air. By strategically positioning inlet and return air grills, workplaces can achieve optimal airflow, preventing stuffiness and promoting better air quality for all occupants.
- **Exposure and Orientation of Windows:** Windows aren't just for admiring the view—they also influence the comfort and energy efficiency of a space. The direction in which windows face can significantly impact the amount of sunlight and heat entering a room. Offices with south-facing windows bask in ample sunlight, which can be a boon in colder climates but may pose challenges in warmer regions, where it can lead to overheating and increased energy consumption. On the flip side, offices with north-facing windows receive more consistent light without the risk of excessive heat, providing a more balanced and comfortable environment for occupants.

- **Insulation of Walls and Roof:** Walls and roofs are more than just structural elements—they're key players in regulating indoor temperature and comfort. Proper insulation is crucial for maintaining a stable and comfortable climate within the workplace. Depending on the office's placement within a building, the roof can act as a constant temperature source, influencing heat transfer within the environment. By ensuring the right insulation levels in walls and roofs, workplaces can minimize heat loss in winter and heat gain in summer, creating a more energy-efficient and comfortable indoor environment year-round. In regions with cooler temperatures where heat loss is an issue, insulation of walls and roofs becomes pertinent for a productive flow of work.

These considerations may seem subtle, but they can make a world of difference in the comfort, health, and productivity of employees. By paying attention to details like air grille placement, window orientation, and insulation, workplaces can create environments that not only look inviting but also feel welcoming and supportive of employees' well-being.

Supporting employees' well-being in terms of mental and emotional health is also paramount, particularly in light of the significant economic impact of conditions like depression and anxiety. According to the World Health Organization (WHO), these issues result in a staggering $1 trillion loss in global productivity annually. While there exist multiple approaches organizations can take to bolster mental well-being, let's explore how workplace design can play a pivotal role in this endeavor.

Color and Materiality:
Colors can influence our mood and mental and physical well-being. Research in neuroscience and psychology has illuminated the profound effect that colors can have on our brains, hormones, mood, behavior, and physiology. Consequently, the colors surrounding us on a daily basis play a pivotal role in shaping our

emotions. This underscores the significance of carefully selecting colors in our workplaces.

Light, composed of various colors, interacts with our retina, transforming into electrical impulses that travel to the hypothalamus. This process influences our hormonal balance. Each color, characterized by distinct wavelengths, interacts with the endocrine system, affecting mood and stress levels in diverse ways.

Color psychology reveals that green, in particular, is a mood-enhancing color renowned for its effectiveness in alleviating stress. Incorporating natural elements like plants can act as buffers between stress triggers and employees. The strategic use of more plants, expansive windows opening to nature, water features, and open spaces contributes to cultivating a healthier and more serene workplace environment.

Circadian lighting:

The circadian rhythm is the body's 24-hour mechanism that impacts the behavioral, biological, and mental processes. It's controlled by the suprachiasmatic nucleus (SCN), a portion of the brain situated just above the optic nerves. It affects productivity, alertness, body temperature, sleep cycle, and digestive system. Although the pineal gland and the SCN mainly regulate the circadian rhythm, environmental factors, specifically light intensity, affect the natural process. When there's abundant light in the morning, it's normal to feel energized; at night, when there's less light in the environment, most people will feel drowsy – this is the circadian rhythm at work.

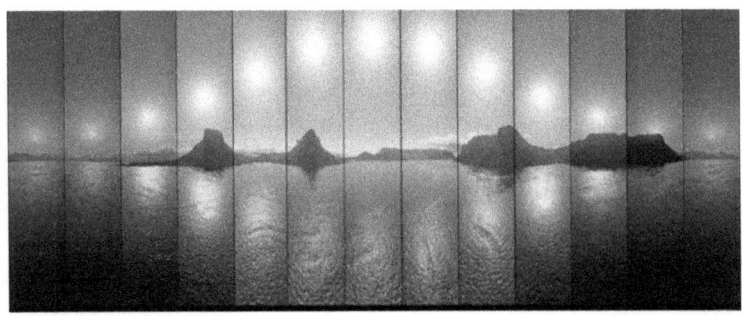

While the body's circadian rhythm responds to the presence of natural light, it does the same for artificial light sources. LED bulbs, smartphones, computers, and TV screens are examples of artificial light sources that emit blue light.

As discussed, the human circadian rhythm depends on the input received by the retinal photoreceptors. These receptors work properly so long as they're not exposed to light sources emitting a wavelength shorter than 450nm. The 450nm to 500nm wavelength interval is where the blue portion of the light spectrum is often found.

A circadian lighting system is designed to replicate the presence of natural light from daytime to nighttime. The color temperature, the light source's angle, and the brightness's intensity are all copied so that the lighting inside a room is in sync with the circadian system. By dynamically tracking the sun's movement, it's possible to recreate the natural light outside the office. A properly installed circadian lighting system can bring several benefits, more than just a good night's sleep. It can increase alertness and concentration, boost the immune system, elevate mood, improve memory and cognitive function, and enhance metabolism.

Circadian lighting products emit bioactive light that helps regulate the circadian rhythm and improve overall productivity. This promise has businesses yearning to install a circadian lighting system to benefit the employees and the enterprise in the long run.

Studies show that people in the workplace exposed to a low blue light source perform up to 25% better than those working under an uncontrollably bright light source.

Creative Engagement

Designing opportunities for creative engagements represents another avenue for cultivating a more joyful workplace. It functions as a type of mindfulness, as involvement in creative pursuits fosters concentration and a state of 'flow'—a total immersion in an activity leading to heightened clarity and tranquility. A plant here, pictures of the family there, and some colorful sticky notes instead of the pop-up notifications could make the work spaces more fun! Recent research has observed that individuals who engage in creative activities experience increased energy levels the following day, sparking a positive domino effect that inspires further creativity.

Recognizing these benefits, numerous workplaces now provide employees with creative workshops. These initiatives serve not only as a means of enhancing team morale and communication but also as a way to promote happiness among staff members. By designing opportunities for creative engagement, workplaces aim to tap into the positive ripple effects of heightened energy, inspiration, and overall well-being.

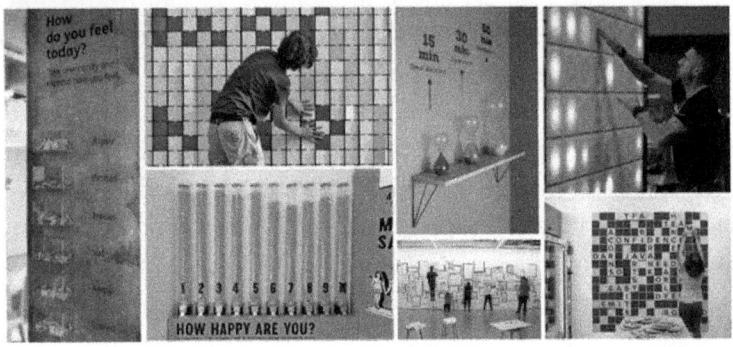

Organizations can prioritize and integrate employee well-being by establishing environments that actively support and encourage it, ensuring that well-being is not an afterthought but a fundamental aspect of workplace design. In this approach, mental health takes a central role in shaping the overall design and atmosphere of the workplace. This perspective recognizes that creating a work environment that promotes well-being is not merely an additional consideration but an essential element for fostering a positive and healthy workplace culture.

Olfactory management

It may sound like a stretch, but did you know the scent of your environment significantly influences how you behave and feel? For example, unwanted smells can be a significant source of frustration.

And pleasant, activating fragrances can improve your concentration, productivity, and mood. Retailers frequently employ scents as a sales tool, especially in supermarkets where enticing smells can prompt customers to make purchases, even if they weren't initially hungry. Research supports the effectiveness of this technique, with studies showing a three-fold increase in the sales of baked goods when the smell of baking bread is released in a supermarket. While using smell as a tool in the office environment is relatively unexplored, and various research sources indicate its potential and significance.

As someone who has extremely sensitive olfactory senses, I recently came across an interesting article that talked about a survey by Savills on what workplaces want. The survey observed that 77% of respondents rated the smell of their office as important. Air Aroma, a leading scent marketing firm, suggests using scenting to create zones within a workspace. Relaxation can be enhanced by using scents that give the illusion of being outside the office.

For example, using a café scent in a breakout area can help take employees out of 'work mode' during breaks and informal meetings. Alternatively, revitalizing scents such as citrus and peppermint can counteract the slump employees may experience after lunch or toward the end of the workday to aid productivity. According to them, people can remember a scent with 65% accuracy after one year, while visual memory sinks to 50% accuracy after a few months. There's significant evidence of the benefits of correctly managing the smell of an office as well as clear demand from office workers.

This final element of office fit-out has long been overlooked, but it's likely to become common practice soon.

More control: Lastly, this is something very simple yet powerful. Research indicates that having little discretion over how work gets done is associated not only with poorer mental health but also with higher rates of heart disease. What's more, the combination of high work demands and low job control significantly increases the risks of stress and cardiovascular issues. Even relatively small changes in worker autonomy can affect employee well-being. How you want to use your workstation on a particular day or where you want to sit at a certain time of the day has to be the user's choice; enabling this flexibility will certainly increase engagement, trust, and overall well-being.

Beyond all, creating a work culture where employees can develop supportive relationships with their colleagues can be an important strategy for increasing employee well-being. Fostering a sense of social belonging doesn't have to be a complex or expensive proposition.

> ### Workplace Wellness; A Case Study: Hewlett-Packard Inc. (HP), Gurgaon, India
>
> Hewlett-Packard (HP) in Gurgaon, India, embarked on a transformative journey with the Futurescapes project, in collaboration with Unispace and its subsidiary, Downstream. This initiative aimed to redefine HP's workplace environment by creating spaces that not only foster AI innovation and collaboration but also prioritize employee well-being. The project successfully merged HP's history and brand identity with modern workplace needs, resulting in four distinct zones: Growthscapes, Socialscapes, Playscapes, and Techscapes.
>
> Key Features Emphasizing Workplace Wellness:
>
> **1. Techscape: Central to Innovation and Collaboration**
>
> - **Design Focus:** The Techscape, designed by Downstream, is the heart of the Futurescapes project. It features dynamic zones such as the Reception, Tech Café, Presentation Area, Theatre, and Lounge, all tailored to promote AI innovation and seamless collaboration.
> - **Wellness Impact:** These zones are designed to support diverse work styles and needs, allowing employees to transition effortlessly between different tasks and interactions. This adaptability not only enhances productivity but also reduces stress, contributing to overall employee well-being.

2. Adaptability and Functionality:

- **Design Focus:** The project placed a strong emphasis on adaptability, incorporating movable digital screens that allow spaces to transition between small demos and large meetings. This design integrates employee and customer areas, optimizing the functionality of the workplace.

- **Wellness Impact:** By creating a versatile environment that can easily adapt to various activities, HP ensured that employees have access to spaces that meet their specific needs, whether for focused work, collaboration, or relaxation. This flexibility supports mental well-being by reducing the physical and psychological strain of working in rigid environments.

3. Sustainability Commitment:

- **Design Focus:** HP's dedication to sustainability was a cornerstone of the Futurescapes project, highlighted by the achievement of LEED Gold certification. The project incorporated eco-friendly features such as green walls with real plants and a motion detection lighting system.
- **Wellness Impact:** The sustainable design elements not only demonstrate HP's environmental responsibility but also create a healthier workspace. Improved air quality, energy efficiency, and the inclusion of natural elements contribute to a calming and rejuvenating work environment, which is essential for employee health and well-being.

The successful implementation of the Techscape and other wellness-centric design elements underscores the importance of a holistic approach to workplace wellness, making HPI a leader in creating environments where employees and innovation thrive.

Is your workplace assisting you in sleeping better?

This is something that came as rather shocking to me as I dove deep, talking to various age groups who are in the workforce today. One single big thing that came up as a pain point was sleep deprivation, to the tune of 1 in 5 people! Of course, we are not talking about the toxic managers or binge-watching Netflix here, although that is a minor aspect of this.

Sleep is not just a daily routine; it's a critical biological factor that influences our health and well-being. It impacts our physical, mental, and emotional functioning, and understanding its role can motivate us to make positive changes in our habits and planning.

A 'chronotype' refers to a person's natural inclination towards being a morning or evening person. Understanding the connection between sleep and performance can help individuals discover optimal habits and plan their days more effectively. Recognizing their chronotype allows people to align their tasks with their natural energy levels to maximize productivity and well-being.

Chronotypes and Performance:

Morning Chronotypes: Often referred to as "larks," these individuals tend to be more ethical and creative and make better investment decisions earlier in the day. Morning chronotypes perform their best high-energy, complicated work in the early hours. They can reserve lower-energy tasks for the afternoon, like emails and administrative work.

Evening Chronotypes: Known as "night owls," these individuals are more alert and productive later in the day and into the evening. They should plan their high-energy tasks for later in the day when they are at their peak performance and handle routine tasks earlier.

Workplace fatigue can negatively affect decision-making, memory, reaction time, efficiency, safety, and overall performance, leading to substantial financial repercussions for organizations, industries, and the broader economy. Importantly, this type of fatigue cannot be entirely mitigated through individual choices alone. Research indicates that conventional working hours do not meet the needs of most individuals. Therefore, it's essential for leaders to take action by implementing targeted, evidence-based strategies and for designers to focus on the latest findings in circadian lighting research. Addressing the stigma around fatigue and exploring flexible work arrangements are also critical steps in this process. As we have learned so far, the younger generations are becoming more conscious of their health, and I would imagine it's time for us to rethink physical and mental well-being at the workplace.

Measuring the Impact of Wellness Initiatives: Strategies for Success

Determining the effectiveness of wellness initiatives is crucial for organizations to ensure they're making meaningful strides in supporting their employees' well-being. Let's explore some key metrics and methods to gauge the success of these programs.

Setting Clear Objectives: A vital first step is establishing clear goals for the wellness program. These objectives should align with desired outcomes, such as boosting productivity, enhancing job satisfaction, reducing absenteeism, and fostering a healthy workplace culture. By defining objectives upfront, organizations can focus their measurement efforts and assess the program's impact more effectively.

- **Surveying Employee Satisfaction:**

Regularly conducting anonymous employee satisfaction surveys provides valuable insights into how well the wellness program is being received. These surveys should inquire about the usefulness, accessibility, and effectiveness of various program components. Combining both quantitative and qualitative questions allows for a comprehensive understanding of employees' perspectives and experiences, guiding improvements where needed.

- **Evaluating Productivity:**

Assessing the impact of wellness programs on productivity involves analyzing key performance indicators like absenteeism rates, presenteeism, and turnover. By comparing pre-program and post-program data, organizations can quantify the program's influence on employee performance and well-being, identifying areas of improvement and success.

- **Benchmarking Against Industry Standards:**

Benchmarking results against industry standards and best practices provides valuable context for evaluating the effectiveness of wellness initiatives. By comparing participation rates, health outcomes, and cost savings to industry benchmarks, organizations gain insights into how their program stacks up against peers and can make informed decisions for continuous improvement.

By employing these strategies, organizations can gain a comprehensive understanding of the effectiveness of their wellness initiatives and make informed decisions to support their employees' well-being.

Unveiling Barriers and Charting Paths to Wellness Success

Implementing workplace wellness programs is like navigating a maze; potential benefits are abundant, but barriers often hinder progress. From financial constraints to employee skepticism, each obstacle presents a unique challenge.

In the quest for wellness, financial hurdles can loom large. While some initiatives come at little cost, others require investment. Securing support from leadership is key to ensuring adequate funding. Plus, incentivizing participation can bolster financial backing and drive engagement.

Imagine having a treasure trove of benefits but no map to find them. A lack of awareness can obscure the path to wellness. Diversifying communication channels, from office info stations to engaging workshops, can illuminate the way and ensure no benefits go unnoticed.

Doubt can cast a shadow on even the brightest wellness initiatives. Convincing employees of a program's efficacy requires solid evidence. Showcasing research-backed benefits and sharing success stories can dispel skepticism and build trust in the program's reliability.

When motives seem murky, participation can wane. Employees may question whether wellness is a genuine priority or just a corporate facade. To foster trust, organizations must align actions with intentions, emphasizing employee well-being as a core value and steering clear of overly corporate messaging.

Navigating these challenges requires more than just a roadmap; it demands innovation, sincerity, and a commitment to employee well- being. By addressing these barriers head-on, organizations can pave the way to a healthier, happier workplace for all.

Nurturing Well-being in Remote and Hybrid Work Environments

As we have realized, the landscape of work has transformed quite a bit, breaking free from the confines of traditional office spaces. Whether it's remote, hybrid, or the next buzzword on the horizon, ensuring employee well-being remains paramount.

- **Adapting to Remote Realities:**

In the absence of a physical workplace, remote workers can grapple with isolation and blurred boundaries. Offering virtual wellness programs and mental health support becomes imperative. Establishing clear communication norms and work-life balance guidelines helps maintain harmony in remote settings.

- **Balancing Act in Hybrid Worlds:**

For those straddling office and remote work, the line between professional and personal life can blur. Burnout lurks where boundaries falter. Providing tools for boundary-setting, fostering connections with colleagues, and supporting mental and physical health is key. Flexibility is the linchpin in balancing the demands of both realms.

- **Tools for Thriving:**
Regardless of the work setting, empowering employees with resources is pivotal. From gym memberships to virtual team meetings, from mental health support to vacation stipends, a plethora of tools exist to enhance health and happiness. HR teams can tap into creativity to curate offerings that cater to diverse needs and preferences.

In this evolving landscape, adaptability and innovation are essential. By embracing the unique challenges and opportunities of remote and hybrid work environments, organizations can cultivate a culture of well-being that transcends physical boundaries and nurtures the holistic health of their workforce.

Leadership's Vital Role in Cultivating Workplace Wellness

Leadership isn't just about hitting targets; it's about fostering thriving teams. Acknowledging the importance of balance and well-being, leaders set the tone for a culture that prioritizes holistic health. Although most of us realize the potential of workplace wellness, it is pertinent to understand and recognize that the implementation of these would be much more effective and simpler if we take the top-down approach. Let us explore how leadership within organizations can support this:

- **Leading by Example:**
Leaders who embody a balanced lifestyle inspire their teams to follow suit. By prioritizing self-care and promoting well-being initiatives, they pave the way for a healthier, more engaged workforce.

- **Integrating Well-being Across the Board:**
From recruitment to retirement, well-being should be woven into every aspect of the employee's journey. Organizations gain a competitive edge by prioritizing work-life balance, mental health support, and ongoing development opportunities.
- **Embracing Flexible Work Arrangements:**
Flexible work options are on the rise, but their success hinges on effective leadership. By championing flexibility and trust, leaders empower employees to achieve a harmonious blend of work and life responsibilities.
- **Destigmatizing Mental Health:**
Leaders play a crucial role in breaking down the barriers surrounding mental health. By fostering a culture of openness and support, they create an environment where employees feel safe to seek help and discuss their challenges without fear of judgment.

In the quest for a healthier, happier workplace, leadership is the guiding light. By championing well-being at every turn, leaders sow the seeds for a culture where employees can thrive personally and professionally.

Now that we have explored the prioritization of employees' well-being in the workplace let's delve into the agile work environment. It's crucial for leaders to champion this innovative approach, as it not only fosters employee well-being but also enhances productivity, promotes work-life balance, and reduces operational costs. The following chapter will delve into the flexibility and adaptability that an agile working environment offers.

7
ALL ABOUT FLEXIBILITY:
EMBRACING AGILE WORK ENVIRONMENT

Imagine a workplace where employees have the freedom to choose when and where they work, where work-life integration is seamlessly incorporated into daily life. In this chapter, we are about to deep dive into the concept of flexibility and its vital role in creating agile work environments that empower employees and drive productivity.

This chapter aims to explore the benefits, challenges, and strategies associated with embracing flexible work arrangements.

We will demonstrate how organizations can design spaces that support mobility, choice, and work-life integration while effectively managing the implementation and maintenance of flexible workplace solutions.

Further, we will discuss the significance of flexibility in today's work landscape and how it contributes to employee satisfaction, engagement, and productivity. We will explore the positive impact of agile work environments through case studies and examples.

Additionally, we will provide practical strategies for implementing and managing flexible workplace solutions while addressing the potential challenges and pitfalls to watch out for.

Flexibility and Workplace Design

If just five years ago, you asked someone the first thing that would pop into their mind after hearing the word 'flexibility,' they'd answer with 'yoga' or 'gymnastics.' Little did they know that someday, flexibility would apply to workplaces and transform the whole professional scene with its revolutionary fundamentals.

We are witnessing a newfound level of independence among younger generations, particularly Gen Z, when it comes to making and controlling their choices. They will no longer accept directions or restrictions from their employers with a straight face. They are highly aware of everything they want in life and, more importantly, what they don't. That is a positive thing since it provides capable and true leaders the chance to give them more agency at work.

As one would expect from a generation that has grown up in a welcoming and accepting environment, they feel empowered to build and express their own unique brand. Gone are the days when employees were either expected or would themselves try to blend with the workspace and become nearly one with the crowd. Now, the younger generation of employees would rather stand out uniquely in the professional world.

While workplace flexibility is not entirely a new concept, the ways it manifests and integrates itself with professional conventions are novel and thrilling. What's fascinating is seeing how the younger generation, known as the 'hypercustom generation' for its obsession with customizing everything they can, makes sense of this newness and expands the definition of flexibility. It is highly likely that GenZ candidates for a job role would rather write their own job descriptions based on what they would like to do and not what they would be required to do.

For example, if we ask them which location they'd prefer to work from home and offer them the options of "work from home," "work from the office," and "others," most of them will check "others" and probably want to work from a beach in the Bahamas. GenZs and Millennials clearly tend to defy classification and instead create their own unique style by combining different elements.

Now, before you start to cringe and form a bad impression about the new workforce, I'd like to change your mind for the better. It is undeniable that this latest brand of professionals comes with a lot of fine print, terms and conditions, and clauses, but that is not a problem at all. Studies have found that GenZs and Millennials are the generations that operate on the principles of continuous improvement and evolution and are not the types to settle and get complacent. They actively ensure that they choose only those fields where they are sure to excel and contribute the most, and then keep upskilling themselves based on changing trends. They are also much more vigilant regarding their rights, so they will ensure that they are not exploited at workplaces while consciously always putting their best foot forward. Quite simply, they are a gift to the professional world in terms of skills, knowledge, attitude, and everything in between. All they want is to receive as much in return as the immense value they create for the organization they are employed in; that is a completely fair ask.

Flexibility is thus one of the most important factors for organizations that want to increase their hiring of young people in order to benefit from a wonderfully capable talent pool. Employees want to be assured that their employers care about their values, priorities, and investments, so the work environment you design for them should mirror the company's stance on flexibility.

When it comes to flexible work, many companies have different interpretations. Some companies' core policies include flexible work, making it a regular part of each employee's schedule. However, some may choose to handle flexitime on an individual basis to meet the needs of their employees. Innovation in the workplace is advancing quickly, regardless of how a company views flexibility. The expectations of modern workers are being raised as flexible work becomes a more integral part of people's lives.

Strong multigenerational teams are beneficial for varied firms, especially in the context of flexible work, and today's workforce comprises three generations: Generation X, Millennials, and Generation Z. Coexisting with older generations who value flextime for family caregiving duties are younger generations that are drawn to remote employment and its flexibility because it fits well with their active lifestyles. The organization benefits from the diverse range of experiences and expertise that this diversity brings. However, some employees can find this flexible structure strange and challenging. The large sample size might cause people to generalize about people's communication preferences based on their initial impressions.

One of the biggest misconceptions that people have about flexible and hybrid work is that it is solely motivated by cost-cutting and that only cash-strapped organizations want their employees to be anywhere but in an office. The decrease in high office real estate expenses relative to pre-pandemic full capacity is undeniably an additional benefit, even if many organizations have embraced remote-first, remote-only, or hybrid methods in response to employee demands. Because of this cost consideration, moving to a hybrid or remote model may be the best option for some businesses. But surely, fewer expenses are not the only reason.

Instead of cutting corners, companies should put their money into making sure their employees have the kind of places they need to work after the pandemic. Funds should be reallocated to focus on strategic investments that meet the changing needs of the workforce rather than spending cuts. I wouldn't be shocked if, in any forward-thinking organization, the function of an office is discovered to be evolving regularly as various teams discover their optimal time, place, and method of operation. Nevertheless, the office space will remain important and serve as a major staple for all employees.

One more prevalent misconception is the idea that giving employees more freedom will lead to lower productivity. This couldn't be further from the truth; abundant evidence shows that workers who can benefit from flexibility are happier, more fulfilled, and significantly more productive. The reason behind this positive consequence is that flexibility doesn't change the core aspects of job obligations or expected outputs. Instead, it modifies the current agreement between the employer and employee to boost compatibility.

Here's one thing I've learned from my experience: the tighter you bind your employees with rules and policies, the more likely it is that all your efforts will backfire and lead to more harm than good. When you intentionally or unintentionally communicate to the workforce that you do not trust them, it is bound to alienate them from the organization and lead to an eventual falling out of processes. Staff members are more likely to be loyal when they are trusted and given the freedom to work when it serves them best. Thus, freedom is a growth booster and not the opposite.

Put simply, when businesses are open to being flexible, it benefits their employees and the company as a whole.

Transitioning to Agile Work Environments

Now, navigating flexibility in the workplace can present challenges in terms of planning, implementation, and sustainability. However, these challenges can be effectively addressed through a strategic approach to flexible arrangements. In this section, we will not only explore the difficulties but also provide solutions for establishing and maintaining a flexible workplace.

Picture this: your firm in India is working with a partner firm in Germany, and you have been struggling to coordinate your interactions due to the time differences. Sometimes, the EOD you had in mind ends up being a day earlier than planned, and this leads to a lot of confusion. When you require urgent responses to emails, either the concerned employees are away or respond later than required. Quite clearly, the issues are endless. It might be difficult to communicate effectively when working with colleagues in different time zones and with hybrid or remote work arrangements. However, there certainly are ways to make asynchronous work more efficient. We will discuss some ways team leaders can make life easier for employees working remotely.

The first step is to consult with staff to find out when they are most receptive to communication. Often, people working remotely ration their working hours into slots for productivity, small breaks, and deeply focused work. When seen as a whole schedule, these slots may or may not match the schedule of other employees, and the possibility of a potential disruption arises. That is why it is necessary to figure out the time slots that employees would be most open to based on their availability and mindset. Another option is for the employers themselves to determine and fix a certain period of the day when every employee should be reachable via phone or email. This way, there will be a uniform structure that is easier to track and manage. Also, give specific examples of when a meeting is necessary and how to choose who should attend; select employees for each kind of meeting required based on relevance, expertise, efficiency, and more. Lastly, technology should be incorporated into the workplace, whether it's an office or a home so that team members can utilize it for internal communication. Instead of holding regular meetings, employers should create short, screen-recorded videos to share feedback.

It's important to remember that holding more meetings won't solve the problem of insufficient face-to-face communication; on the contrary, it might discourage staff from working efficiently. The quality of meetings is also important; instead of daily status updates, try having fun team-building and collaboration meetings once a week to get everyone involved.

Now, what if we're referring to a company that is currently developing its own culture? Although they have many benefits, such as reduced expenses, from flexible work arrangements, they also run the risk of undermining company culture. One risk is the potential for a divide to emerge between remote and in-office employees, leading to feelings of isolation or disconnection. Without regular face-to-face interactions, people working remotely may miss out on spontaneous conversations, team bonding activities, and more such opportunities that contribute to a strong sense of camaraderie and belonging within the company. The lively workplace atmosphere that is typically enhanced by frequent in-person encounters and casual chatter could be dampened in a mixed work arrangement. Moreover, a shift towards remote work may impact the company's ability to nurture its desired culture and core values, too.

To maintain a strong and cohesive work culture, it is important to create opportunities for hybrid team-building activities, promote constant communication, and celebrate significant milestones. Online games, virtual coffee breaks, and virtual happy hours are all examples of virtual team-building activities that can help members of distant teams connect and form bonds. Formal and informal team meetings should be held on a regular basis to allow for a free flow of information and ideas. Raising morale and fostering a pleasant work culture are two outcomes that can be achieved through commemorating and recognizing milestones, whether they pertain to personal victories or project accomplishments.

To carry our discussion forward, establishing a flexible work schedule requires more than just letting people come and go from the office whenever they like. Consideration of specific work duties and needs necessitates a methodical and personalized strategy. Without effective implementation and enough training for every employee, the well-intentioned shift toward work flexibility could devolve into anarchy. Here are some ways to maximize your flexibility at work without sacrificing quality or productivity.

Clearly defining expectations and rules that are specific to the demands of various roles within the organization is essential for establishing a successful framework for work flexibility. This involves recognizing that not all positions can operate under the same flexibility parameters and thus customizing flexibility options accordingly. Employees should be provided with comprehensive training and support to effectively navigate the challenges of flexible work arrangements, including clarifications on remote collaboration tools, time management, and communication strategies. Open communication channels between employees and management should be fostered to address concerns and provide feedback, ensuring a supportive environment for all. Clear performance metrics should also be established and regularly reviewed to maintain output quality and productivity standards. Then, leveraging technology to create an efficient virtual work environment is also essential, with investments in collaborative tools, better communication, and project management for remote and flexible teams. Additionally, trial periods for flexibility arrangements can be beneficial to assess their effectiveness and make necessary adjustments before committing to long-term changes. Lastly, offering a range of flexibility options based on individual and job-specific needs empowers employees to choose arrangements that best suit their circumstances, ultimately contributing to a more adaptable and cohesive workforce.

To improve their efficiency and productivity, agile teams can make use of a plethora of tools and resources. The most common ones include programs that help manage projects, collaborate on them, and keep tabs on their progress. Tools for project management software make it easier to organize and carry out tasks. Features for scheduling, resource allocation, and task management are provided, guaranteeing a unified approach to project operations. Team members are able to communicate and work together more effectively using collaborative platforms such as Slack and Microsoft Teams. They provide ways for video conferencing, file sharing, and real-time texting, which facilitates easy collaboration. The use of these resources allows agile teams to work together better, simplify project management, and keep track of their progress more easily, all of which lead to better project outcomes.

By carefully considering these strategies, organizations can navigate the implementation of work flexibility in a way that aligns with their specific needs and priorities while maintaining a focus on work quality and productivity.

The ability to recruit, retain, and support talent—regardless of gender, role, or anything else, depends on equitable flexibility, which in turn unlocks the full potential of human capital. Achieving fair flexibility requires actions that are both intentional and well-planned. This goes beyond the scope of workplace design and into creating an organization-wide strategy. Employees with more leeway in their work schedules report higher levels of personal and organizational efficiency and productivity and a better work-life balance.

When asked how to make the workplace more equitable, employees ranked flexibility as the most effective strategy, followed by leadership initiatives, unbiased promotion methods, and recruitment policies. When carefully planned, flexibility can empower workers, giving them control over their career advancement, work hours, and availability. However, it can have devastating results. Many workers see the restrictions on their ability to advance in their careers, the longer hours they are expected to work, and the constant assumption that they must always be available as major negatives of flexible work arrangements. The significance of careful execution in maximizing the benefits of flexibility while avoiding its negatives is underscored by the fact that perception difficulties may also develop.

Flexibility must be carefully and intentionally constructed to avoid unintended consequences. To achieve this, it is necessary to define success precisely, include the views of stakeholders and minority groups, delegate decision-making power to key team members, and incentivize simplicity and efficient implementation. Creating a welcoming and inclusive workplace relies heavily on thoughtfully crafting policies that allow equitable flexibility, and this is a responsibility that falls on the shoulders of leadership. Their commitment to this cause can inspire and motivate the entire organization.

Benefits of Self-Understanding and Flexible Scheduling

Understanding the importance of flexibility in the workplace, we can now explore the benefits of incorporating self-understanding and flexible scheduling. Organizations can foster a more productive, satisfied, and inclusive work environment by enabling employees to better understand their needs and offering flexible scheduling options. Let's delve into these benefits in more detail.

Optimizing Daily Routines:
- **High-Energy Tasks:** By identifying when they are most alert, individuals can schedule complex and high-energy tasks during these peak times for better efficiency and effectiveness.
- **Routine Tasks:** Understanding when their energy wanes allows individuals to plan less demanding tasks, such as responding to emails and handling administrative work, during these periods. This self-awareness can lead to a more enlightened approach to task management.
- **Enhanced Productivity:** Flexible work hours allow individuals to work during their most productive times, leading to improved performance and job satisfaction.

- **Time Savings:** Flexible schedules can help employees avoid peak traffic times, saving time and reducing stress associated with commuting.

The Future of Flexibility

As we have witnessed, accommodating employees of all ages in the workplace is now essential. Millennials and younger generations highly value flexible work schedules when deciding where to work. Flexible work arrangements are a smart move for businesses since they encourage more employees to take part in the workforce, which helps build stronger economies. To recruit a more diverse pool of candidates, businesses should provide flexible work arrangements so that employees can meet their specific requirements and preferences. Participation in the workforce is increased as a whole due to this inclusiveness.

Adapting to ever-changing environments will require the capacity to constantly learn new things and put those talents to use. As AI and other technologies revolutionize the way we work, it is crucial for individuals to prioritize skill upskilling, adaptability, and diversity in their skill sets. For the younger generation, in particular, who are attempting to thrive in this dynamic and fast-evolving setting.

If a firm takes an all-or-nothing approach to figuring out how to lead or work in the workplace of the future, it may not be able to adapt and survive in a world that is becoming more unpredictable, volatile, and uncertain. It seems like working remotely is here to stay, according to all the research. Having the freedom to choose one's own schedule, location, and methods of work is highly prized by professionals, and remote work offers just that.

To be sure, online conversations have their place, but nothing beats face-to-face meetings when it comes to building rapport, understanding, and friendships. There is a chance to foster a new performance culture and meet the demands of a varied workforce by making the switch to a hybrid or flexible office. As a development from the conventional methods of doing business, this culture is defined by openness, tolerance, and respect for all members of the team. An adaptive and dynamic corporate culture may flourish when businesses embrace flexibility and use it to their advantage, reaping the benefits of both remote and in-person employment.

The question of how our companies are going to accommodate a new wave of digital natives who want greater autonomy, room to grow professionally, and technology to showcase their skills becomes more pressing in light of conversations regarding the future of work.

When it is your turn to delve into the world of flexible work arrangements, I encourage you to assess the needs and preferences of your workforce and consider how incorporating flexibility can benefit your organization. Take the insights and strategies this chapter shares and implement small changes to create an agile work environment. It's important to monitor the impact of these changes, gather feedback from employees, and continuously refine your approach. By embracing flexibility and continuously refining your approach, you can unlock a new level of productivity and employee satisfaction within your organization.

As you explore the possibilities of flexible work arrangements and their impact on workplace dynamics, you are primed to take the next step: preparing for the future of our workspaces. It is essential to understand and embrace the digital age in the workplace, as it is a key factor in shaping the future of work. Let us move on to embracing the digital wave that has swept over the next-gen workplaces.

8
EMBRACING THE DIGITAL AGE
IN THE WORKPLACE

EMBRACING THE DIGITAL AGE IN THE WORKPLACE

Step into the office, coffee cup in hand, and let the whirring computers and buzzing servers welcome you. Gone are the days of dusty filing cabinets and cluttered desks; we're plunging headfirst into a bold new era where the currency is bytes, and innovation is king.

In this brave new world, technology isn't just a tool – it's a game-changer. It's reshaping the workplace landscape to put employee happiness, well-being, and fulfillment front and center.

Picture this: every technological marvel, from intelligent assistants to seamless virtual collaboration tools, is meticulously designed to elevate your work experience. It's no longer solely about boosting productivity; it's about instilling a deep sense of purpose and empowerment in every team member.

In this digital realm, technology isn't intimidating; it's liberating. It's your trusty sidekick, streamlining tasks and turning the mundane into the marvelous. We've bid farewell to the days of fax machines and snail mail – even email seems passé in the face of the cutting-edge technologies that now grace our workplace.

The impact of technology on the workplace is nothing short of revolutionary. It infiltrates every facet of our work lives, from communication to the tools we wield to conquer our daily challenges.

These technological marvels come in two distinct flavors: those that face the workforce directly and those that support the workplace infrastructure itself. From instant messaging apps to sleek room-booking software, workplace-facing technologies empower employees to excel. Meanwhile, behind the scenes, occupancy sensors and Integrated Workplace Management Systems (IWMS) lay the foundation for a seamlessly integrated digital workplace ecosystem.

Together, these technologies form the beating heart of the modern workplace, driving efficiency, fostering collaboration, and nurturing employee satisfaction. As technology continues to evolve at breakneck speed, so will how it enriches and transforms the workplace experience for employees worldwide.

Welcome to the digital revolution – where the only constant is innovation, and the possibilities are endless.

Why the Tech Frenzy?

A salesperson or an accountant today might have a job title similar to those of decades past, but their daily grind involves a world of difference. This transformation is fueled by the rapid growth of workplace technology, bringing sophistication to every corner of our professional lives.

Enhanced Interpersonal Communication

Technology has revolutionized how we connect, speeding up the pace and expanding the scope of our interactions. Just take the shift from email to messaging apps, for example.

Imagine Jim needs to reach out to Sally about a project. Instead of waiting for an email reply, he shoots her an instant message through Slack. Sally receives the message instantly, and they have a quick back-and-forth in a shared channel. No more buried emails or endless chains—just clear, instant communication keeps everyone on the same page.

Streamlined Workflows

But it's not just about chatting faster; technology has also turbocharged our workflows. With the help of workplace planning and coordination software like IWMS and CAFM platforms, tasks that used to take days or weeks can now be completed in minutes.

Bob and John don't need to twiddle their thumbs waiting for a meeting space to free up—they can find or create an alternative space in seconds. And Steve can reserve a workspace online with just a few clicks, streamlining his day like never before.

Access Anywhere, Anytime

Ah, the wonders of the cloud! This game-changing technology has granted us access to our digital assets anywhere. Need to pull up a presentation for a meeting on the fly? No problem. With a few clicks, it's right there at your fingertips.

Boosting Productivity

And let's not forget the elephant in the room: productivity. Technology has been the driving force behind our ability to work smarter, not harder. Imagine tackling your daily tasks without a computer, email, or messaging apps—it's practically unthinkable!

From communicating to collaborating, technology permeates every aspect of our work lives, revolutionizing how, where, and when we get things done. And as technology continues to evolve, so will our ability to adapt, innovate, and thrive in the ever-changing landscape of the modern workplace.

So, why all this tech? Because in today's fast-paced world, it's not just about keeping up—it's about staying ahead of the curve and redefining what's possible.

How Technology Revolutionized the Workplace?

In the blink of an eye, the modern workplace has undergone a complete makeover, thanks to the whirlwind of technological advancements that have reshaped the landscape. In just two short decades, we've witnessed a metamorphosis that has altered how, where, and when we work.

- **Remote Work:** Perhaps the most glaring transformation, technology has liberated work from the confines of traditional office spaces. With the advent of cloud computing and lightning-fast internet, employees now have the freedom to work from virtually anywhere, ushering in an era of flexibility and work-life harmony.
- **Communication and Collaboration:** Platforms like Slack, Microsoft Teams, and Zoom have shattered communication barriers, facilitating seamless teamwork regardless of geographical boundaries. Meetings, brainstorming sessions, and

project collaborations now happen in real-time, with just a few clicks.

- **Boosting Efficiency and Productivity:** AI and automation have taken over mundane tasks, from tedious data entry to repetitive customer service inquiries, allowing human resources to redirect their focus towards more creative and strategic pursuits.
- **Data-Driven Decision Making:** Armed with cutting-edge analytics tools, businesses can harness the power of big data to make informed decisions, predict market trends, and tailor services to meet customers' evolving needs.
- **Elevated Importance:** As our reliance on digital platforms intensifies, so does the urgency for robust cybersecurity measures. Safeguarding sensitive data against cyber threats has emerged as a top priority for businesses, ensuring the trust and confidence of customers and stakeholders alike.
- **Impact on Employee Skills and Training:** The technological revolution has shifted the demand for skills, emphasizing digital literacy, problem-solving, and adaptability. Employers increasingly invest in continuous learning and development programs to keep their workforce abreast of technological advancements.
- **The Future of Work:** With the rise of the Internet of Things (IoT) and the dawn of smart offices, workplaces are poised to become even more efficient and employee-centric. Meanwhile, AI's expanding role in decision-making and personalized customer experiences offers a glimpse into a future where technology plays an even more central role.

The impact of technology on the modern workplace is nothing short of revolutionary. It has transformed how we work and has laid the groundwork for a more interconnected, efficient, and adaptable work environment. As we embrace this digital era, the challenge lies in finding the delicate balance between technological progress and maintaining a human-centered approach to work.

Digital transformation isn't just a technological upgrade—it's a fundamental shift in how businesses operate and compete in the digital era. By embracing digital transformation, companies can unlock new opportunities for growth, innovation, and success in an increasingly digital world.

What are some examples of digital tools and solutions that can enhance the workplace experience?

We're immersed in a digitally driven era, where companies increasingly pivot towards digitizing their operations. An overwhelming 91% of businesses are spearheading digital projects, marking a shift from traditional cubicle setups to more fluid work arrangements like open floor plans, remote work setups, and flexible schedules. In this dynamic landscape, the seamless integration of technology and design becomes paramount to meet evolving employee needs.

Yet, navigating the vast array of available technology can feel like traversing a labyrinth. Embracing the tech wave demands adopting new tools and ushering in a paradigm shift in leveraging data and technology to enhance operations and team performance. Selecting the right app solutions is pivotal for transitioning to a digital workplace. However, the real challenge lies in ensuring every investment made is scalable and enduring, considering the rapid pace at which these cutting-edge resources evolve—sometimes faster than users can keep up.

Let's delve into a few key innovations reshaping the modern workplace:
- **Optimized Digital Toolkit:** Beyond basic collaboration tools, state-of-the-art technological platforms empower employees to function seamlessly regardless of location. Optimizing and integrating these digital tools in today's landscape isn't just a perk - — it's a necessity.

- **Hyperflexible Conferencing:** The onset of the pandemic accelerated the reliance on personal communication tools, leading to the rise of Bring Your Device (BYOD) strategies. BYOD offers flexibility in how, where, and when employees collaborate, catering to the growing mobility expectations among employees and employers. Successful implementation hinges on adeptly introducing BYOD into corporate resources while streamlining user processes.
- **AI & Automation:** Love or loathe them, AI and automation have permeated virtually every facet of the business world. From virtual note-taking tools to productivity-boosting virtual assistants like Grammarly, Chat GPT, Claude, Flex from Grok, Meta, and Google Gemini, to name a few, AI-driven solutions offer immense potential for companies to harness. As these technologies take center stage, companies are poised to tap into unprecedented efficiencies and innovations.

As we navigate this digital frontier, adapting to these transformative technologies isn't just about staying ahead—it's about reshaping how we work and collaborate in the modern age.

How Can Organizations Harness Technology to Meet the Expectations of Younger Generations?

The priorities of younger generations in the workplace often distinguish them from their older counterparts. While they may share some values, they also grapple with unique challenges, particularly those from entering the workforce amidst a global pandemic and economic downturn—a novel experience for many.

Consider Generation Z, for instance. Raised with the internet at their fingertips, they prioritize its role in their learning and career growth. Unlike previous generations, Generation Z fully embraces technology in the workplace, easily driving innovation and efficiency. Despite potential drawbacks, smartphones offer unparalleled connectivity and serve as invaluable tools in the workplace.

Employees can access their entire work setup from any device equipped with many productivity apps, video conferencing platforms like Zoom, AI applications, time-tracking tools, note-taking apps, team communication platforms, and scheduling calendars. This simplifies operations and fosters adaptability and proficiency in diverse communication methods among employees.

The benefits of a tech-savvy workforce are manifold—improved accessibility, heightened productivity, a culture of innovation, and reduced stress are just a few.

Additionally, millennials, another technologically adept generation, place great importance on work-life balance and mental health. To boost morale in the workplace while catering to their preferences, organizations can:

- **Utilize technology as a communication tool:** Leveraging technology for communication can greatly benefit Gen Z employees, who prioritize mental health. Employers can introduce various apps and integrated technologies within the workspace to solicit firsthand feedback—an aspect highly valued by this generation.
- **Facilitate ease and flexibility with technology:** Given their proficiency with technology and apps, younger employees will likely maximize their use of new tools. Allowing them to integrate tech gadgets into their workspace demonstrates trust and encourages innovation within the company.
- **Enhance transparency and visibility through technology:** From sharing the company's vision to providing insight into day-to-day operations, younger generations appreciate transparency. Integrated messaging platforms and dashboards ensure that information is accessible to all employees, moving away from the era when such knowledge was confined to senior executives.

As the public sector endeavors to attract and retain its workforce, modern technology presents an opportunity to cultivate more productive and engaged teams across various government agencies.

Revolutionizing Learning & Development

Consider the pivotal role of learning and development (L&D) in nurturing employee engagement. Instead of relegating L&D to a one-off event during onboarding or an annual compliance checkbox, agency leaders must embrace more dynamic and continuous approaches.

Rather than viewing L&D as a mere cost of employee onboarding, organizations should recognize it as an investment in employee retention. When L&D is integrated seamlessly into the organizational framework and delivered consistently, employees exhibit heightened levels of engagement and productivity. Studies indicate that offering training sessions every 3-6 months strikes a harmonious balance, with employees showing a strong preference for online self-paced learning formats.

According to LinkedIn's 2022 workplace learning report, opportunities for learning and growth have emerged as the primary driver of a positive workplace culture—a significant shift from its previous position at #9 in 2019.

Moreover, L&D resonates with employees of all age groups, albeit for varying reasons. While younger employees perceive it as a means to advance their careers internally or achieve long-term goals, older employees view it as essential for staying updated on industry developments. Beyond job-specific training, employees also seek professional and life skills development, including leadership, mental health and well-being, and self-management.

Enhancing the Training Experience

Managers play a crucial role in improving the employee training experience by acknowledging and accommodating individual learning styles. Providing personalized, flexible, self-paced training options and offering one-on-one coaching or mentoring can significantly enhance engagement and skill development.

In today's competitive labor market, up-skilling or re-skilling existing employees to address skills gaps within government agencies is paramount. A 2023 LinkedIn Learning Report found that 64% of L&D professionals said that reskilling the current workforce to fill skills gaps is now a priority. This represents a significant shift towards internal talent development. This may sometimes involve hiring new employees with baseline skills and providing additional training to fill any skill gaps during onboarding.

Transforming Work Environments with Smart Technology

The surge in adoption of smart home technology and the Internet of Things (IoT) is rapidly reshaping how we live and work. While many American households boast a plethora of smart devices, workplaces are catching up. Leveraging IoT technology, smart office solutions aim to create more comfortable, productive, and healthy work environments. These solutions regulate temperature, lighting, and air quality while offering ergonomic features like smart furniture and adjustable desks. Moreover, IoT-powered scheduling tools and room sensors optimize meeting room utilization, providing insights into organizational meeting patterns and facilitating better space allocation. Additionally, IoT aids sustainability efforts by monitoring energy usage and automating power management for appliances, leading to cost savings.

Facilitating Collaboration with IoT and Asynchronous Tools

As remote and hybrid work models become increasingly prevalent, effective collaboration tools are crucial for maintaining productivity and engagement. IoT and asynchronous collaboration tools offer solutions to bridge the gap between in-person and remote team members. Asynchronous collaboration allows contributions to projects in real-time, promoting autonomy and reducing reliance on hyper-responsive communication channels like email or instant messaging. Managers can mitigate workplace stress and burnout by fostering a culture that values asynchronous communication while enhancing team engagement and productivity.

Embracing Technology: Overcoming Hesitancy and Fostering Engagement

Introducing technology into the workplace can be met with hesitancy, especially regarding corporate surveillance and privacy concerns. Agency leaders must address these apprehensions by reframing technology as a tool for empowerment rather than surveillance. By highlighting the tangible benefits of technology, such as enhanced productivity and collaboration, leaders can cultivate a culture where technology is embraced as a facilitator of engagement and innovation. This shift in perspective enables organizations to harness the full potential of technology while addressing employee concerns about privacy and surveillance.

Why should organizations embrace workplace digitization, and what advantages does it offer employees and employers?

Technology is pivotal in maintaining organizations' strategic advantage in today's competitive landscape. Embracing digital workspaces benefits employees and yields significant advantages for management. For instance, businesses prioritizing digitalization have reported a remarkable reduction in occupancy costs, with up to 30% savings.

According to Deloitte's 2023 Connectivity and Mobile Trends survey, 56% of employed adults work from home at least some of the time. This breaks down as follows:
- 22% work fully from home;
- 34% maintain a hybrid schedule;
- 44% work fully in the office.

This data supports the statement that a majority of employed individuals prefer some form of remote work arrangement. Consequently, they express higher satisfaction with their remote work decision.

However, this positive sentiment is marred by numerous complaints concerning technology. Despite their satisfaction with remote work, many employees encounter difficulties operating work systems and accessing them from home. This trend highlights the lag in technology advancement compared to employees' adaptability, emphasizing the need for a revamped digital approach. But what exactly does this entail, and where should business leaders begin?

Should Every Company Invest in a Digital Workplace?

Amidst the prevalent trend of companies implementing return-to-office (RTO) policies, there's a concurrent reduction in office space. Approximately 82% of businesses express concerns about maintaining their current office setup. Nearly 80% of businesses have downsized since the pandemic, leading to a demand for innovative office utilization strategies. Mandating employees to return to the office is perceived as a temporary fix rather than a comprehensive solution.

For example, Meta's employees, forced to return to the office under RTO policies, encountered challenges due to limited office space availability, including conference rooms, personal desks, and privacy essential for focused work. This unfavorable working environment significantly impacted productivity.

In this scenario, a hybrid workplace emerges as a pragmatic alternative. It allows employees to reconsider office space utilization while ensuring high performance and cost-effectiveness. Almost 89% of CEOs facilitating hybrid-friendly conditions attribute their cost savings to embracing hybrid work models, fostering optimism about cultivating a hybrid workplace culture.

However, for a hybrid environment to thrive, there must be a way to connect in-office and remote employees, providing access to essential features, tools, and communication channels. This is where a digital workplace proves invaluable.

Consequently, any company aiming to establish a proactive and efficient hybrid workplace environment must invest in a digital platform.

Advantages of Developing a Custom Digital Workplace:

A prevalent misconception suggests that readily available messaging platforms, collaborative tools, and video conferencing software like Zoom adequately meet the needs of remote workers in any organization. However, these off-the-shelf solutions often fail to address an enterprise's specific requirements or provide the necessary agility.

It's essential to acknowledge that enterprise growth is dynamic, and solutions must adapt to evolving challenges while aligning with employee needs. Many pre-made tools encounter limitations or cannot support this level of flexibility.

In contrast, a custom digital workplace framework is typically designed with scalability in mind. It equips employees with future-ready features and prepares enterprises for resilience and consistent performance, regardless of shifts in their operational landscape.

Advantages of a Digital Workplace Fueling Enterprise Resilience:

When considering the development of a digital workplace, business leaders and executives should focus on several value-building advantages that will give them a significant competitive edge.

- **Enhanced Flexibility:** Resilience and flexibility are intertwined, making a modern digital workplace essential for businesses aiming to build long-term resilience. One of its primary strengths lies in its ability to streamline complex, multi-step processes, accelerating them and enabling employees to manage them easily from any location without being tied to a specific office.

- **Reduced Dependence on Location:** As major city centers see a decline in population due to people moving to more affordable suburban areas, digital workplaces alleviate transportation concerns. Utilizing a digital workplace platform allows professionals to work from their preferred location effortlessly, saving time and costs associated with commuting.

- **Increased Employee Engagement:** Enhanced accessibility and flexibility significantly contribute to higher employee engagement. The diverse range of hybrid work models enabled by digital workplaces allows businesses to tailor work environments to meet individual employee needs, aligning with their unique performance patterns. This shift empowers employees with greater control over their schedules, increasing engagement in enterprise processes.

- **Preparedness for Unexpected Events:** Despite business leaders' belief that another disruption akin to the COVID-19 pandemic is unlikely, global uncertainties advise against such assumptions. To maintain operational continuity, businesses must be prepared to transition to fully remote work without delay—a capability facilitated by a digital workplace strategy.

- **Mitigating Talent Shortages:** Digital workplaces transcend the boundaries of connecting remote and in-office employees. They enable companies to tap into global talent pools, swiftly integrate new experts into their environment, and onboard them within days. This capability is invaluable, especially considering the growing trend of skill-based hiring in 2024.

Considering these benefits, investing in digital workplace technology equips enterprises with enhanced workflow management, security, and flexibility, positioning them to embrace the future of work confidently.

What Potential Challenges and Risks Does Workplace Digitization Pose?

While workplace digitization offers numerous benefits to organizations, it also brings significant associated risks. Before implementing a digital solution, it's crucial to identify these risks and develop effective measures to mitigate them. Here are some of the most common challenges:

Increased Vulnerability to Cyber-Attacks: Implementing a highly digital workplace expands the potential attack surface for cybercriminals, especially in scenarios like remote work or Bring Your Device (BYOD). Personal devices used for work and heightened susceptibility to social engineering attacks pose significant concerns. Additionally, a fully integrated system in an office setting means a missed security update or a lapse in-app security could expose the system to potential breaches. Robust cybersecurity measures and asset management systems are essential to mitigate these risks effectively.

Privacy Concerns: Organizations may struggle to balance maintaining employee privacy and enhancing the productivity promised by digital workplace solutions. Intruding on employee privacy is a risk, particularly in remote work settings. Establishing clear policies and effective communication channels is crucial to address these concerns.

Impact on Real Connections: Employees risk opting for technology-mediated interactions over in-person gatherings in a completely digital workplace. Personal connections between colleagues are vital in fostering better teams and smoother collaborations. A purely digital workplace may compromise these connections, highlighting the importance of balancing digital and in-person interactions.

While digital workplaces offer numerous benefits to organizations, they also pose significant risks that must be addressed before implementation. Understanding these risks and implementing measures to mitigate them is crucial.

In today's rapidly evolving business landscape, successfully implementing workplace digitization initiatives has become imperative for organizations striving to stay competitive and adapt to changing market dynamics. Let's explore a few notable success stories of companies that have effectively leveraged digital technologies to transform their workplaces:

Microsoft Corporation: Microsoft is a prime example of a company at the forefront of workplace digitization. Through its Microsoft 365 suite, including tools like Teams, SharePoint, and OneDrive, Microsoft has enabled seamless collaboration, communication, and document management for its employees worldwide. This digital workplace solution has improved productivity and streamlined workflows, facilitating remote work, especially during the COVID-19 pandemic.

Siemens: Siemens, a multinational conglomerate, has harnessed workplace digitization to optimize its manufacturing processes and enhance operational efficiency. With its "Industry 4.0" initiative, Siemens integrates digital technologies such as IoT, AI, and automation into its factories to enable predictive maintenance, real-time monitoring, and data-driven decision-making. This digital transformation has enabled Siemens to reduce downtime, increase productivity, and deliver superior products to its customers, thereby maintaining its competitive edge in the market.

These success stories underscore the transformative power of workplace digitization in driving innovation, improving productivity, and fostering agility in today's digital-first world. As organizations continue to navigate the complexities of the modern business environment, embracing digital technologies is essential for staying ahead of the curve and achieving long-term success.

An example of digital optimization to the peak of its intended purpose is Citi Bank, and here's why: So, here's the scoop on how Citi, the multinational investment bank and financial services corporation, jazzed up its workplace game in Chennai, India. Facing the fast-paced shifts in their industry, they knew they needed a fresh office vibe to keep up. So, they went big – 69,000 square feet big – crafting a space that's not just cool but super adaptable and packed with top-notch tech.

Their goal? To reel in the brightest digital minds and set themselves up for long-term success. And let me tell you, they nailed it!

Here's the lowdown:

- Staff at Citi's Chennai office are riding the wave of digital innovation and tech, putting them firmly in the driver's seat of their workplace journey.

- They've cracked the code on scalability and employee wellness by embracing activity-based working and wellness-focused design.

- And guess what? Post-occupancy studies are singing their praises, noting a boost in productivity, collaboration, and those all-important social connections. It's a win-win!

Say hello to the game-changer: 'Citiworks Enterprise – Workplace of the Future.' This cutting-edge office isn't just a place to work – it's a playground for innovation and experimentation. Here, Citi teams are breaking molds, challenging norms, and shaping the future of banking.

Organizations must remain agile, adaptable, and open to change as we move into an increasingly digital future. By embracing digital transformation as a journey rather than a destination, businesses can stay ahead of the curve, drive innovation, and deliver exceptional value to employees and customers. Through effective leadership, clear communication, and a commitment to continuous learning and improvement, organizations can confidently navigate the complexities of workplace digitization and achieve sustainable success in the digital age.

In the upcoming chapter, we will delve into the evolving landscape of emerging trends that organizations need to consider in order to stay ahead of the curve. Get ready to embrace change and design a workplace that is future-proof.

9
MAKING OFFICES FUTUREPROOF

When envisioning the future of work, what comes to mind? Will offices evolve to resemble those of today, or will we see a rise of factories dominated by robots? Perhaps the future will bring entirely new work environments.

Although predicting the future with complete certainty is impossible, it's evident that the nature of work is evolving, mirroring broader global changes. By examining upcoming shifts in work dynamics and trends influencing both the workforce and workspaces, you or your organization can better prepare for what lies ahead.

Building Responsibly

Building sustainable workplaces is like designing a trendy outfit - you want it to be stylish now, but you also don't want it to be so last season by tomorrow! Picture this: you've got your office space all decked out with the latest gadgets and snazzy furniture, only to find out it's about as relevant as a flip phone in a smartphone world.

With the digital revolution turning our work lives upside down faster than you can say "Ctrl+Alt+Delete" and the pandemic throwing office dynamics into a blender, workplaces need to be as adaptable as a chameleon on a dance floor. But let's face it: some workplaces are too stubborn when it comes to change. They stick to their outdated structures like a doggo glued to its favorite toy- no matter how many new toys you get them, they still choose to play with that one old torn or broken piece of toy.

Take India's bustling construction scene, for example. Towers rise, but often without foresight into their future relevance. We're witnessing an era where flashy fit-outs fade faster than the buildings themselves, leaving behind a legacy of wasted resources and missed opportunities.

When it comes to fit-out construction, the increasing prices of raw materials are a major concern, putting additional strain on the environment. For instance, global steel demand alone is projected to increase by 50 % by 2025, highlighting the growing pressure on finite resources and the urgent need for sustainable practices in workplace design and construction. The good news is that a new model is emerging where resources are utilized to their fullest extent, aiming to retain their value for as long as possible. This approach emphasizes sustainability and circularity, focusing on prolonging the lifespan of materials and minimizing waste. The emerging model aims to offer office occupiers increased flexibility while also creating demand for reclaimed or remanufactured components. This shift not only fosters sustainability but also stimulates the growth of new industries while simultaneously reducing waste.

Yes, new buildings can indeed be designed with adaptable structures that endure. Designing buildings with adaptability in mind allows for easier refitting or refurbishing in the future rather than starting from scratch. While retrofitting or refurbishing existing buildings can present challenges, it also offers significant advantages. Across the world, there are numerous examples where designers and developers have successfully converted obsolete buildings into attractive places to live and work, showcasing the potential of adaptive reuse. This approach aligns with the future of sustainable urban development and promotes resource efficiency by maximizing the use of existing infrastructure.

Think about it: buildings designed to evolve alongside our needs, minimizing the need for costly overhauls. And let's not overlook the beauty of adaptive reuse—transforming dilapidated spaces into vibrant hubs of activity. It's not just eco-friendly; it's the future of urban development.

So, let's reimagine our workplaces as more than just bricks and mortar. Let's weave sustainability into their very fabric, creating spaces that inspire, innovate, and endure—a testament to our commitment to both progress and preservation.

In envisioning the future of workplace design, one cannot overlook the pivotal role of Diversity, Equity, Inclusion, and Belonging (DEIB). These aren't just buzzwords; they're the bedrock of a thriving, harmonious work environment. Diversity isn't just about ticking boxes; it's about unlocking the full spectrum of human potential and fostering creativity, innovation, and empathy.

Imagine a workplace where every design element reflects the beauty of identities, where cultural nuances, gender perspectives, and neurodiversity are not just accommodated but celebrated. Such an environment isn't just inclusive; it's a catalyst for organizational success.

At the heart of this lies the understanding that every individual brings a unique set of experiences, talents, and perspectives to the table. By integrating diverse design elements into the very fabric of the workplace, organizations can cultivate an atmosphere where their employees will feel valued, respected, and empowered to be their authentic selves.

Take, for instance, designing for neurodiversity—an area gaining increasing recognition. Conditions like ADHD, ASD, and dyslexia are not deficits but variations in the human experience, each offering its own unique strengths.

By creating spaces that cater to different sensory needs—quiet areas for focused work, calming lighting, and ordered symmetry—organizations can unlock the full potential of neurodivergent individuals. These inclusive design elements not only benefit neurodiverse employees but also enhance focus, reduce sensory overload, and ultimately boost productivity for all.

Moreover, an inclusive workplace isn't just about physical design; it's about fostering a culture of respect and understanding. By championing diversity in all its forms, organizations can tap into a wealth of perspectives, driving creativity, innovation, and, ultimately, organizational success.

When employees feel seen, heard, and valued, they're more likely to collaborate effectively, problem-solve creatively, and drive the business forward.

In the ever-evolving landscape of work, where talent is scarce and competition fierce, creating an inclusive workplace isn't just a moral imperative—it's a strategic advantage. Organizations that embrace diversity in their design and culture will attract top talent and cultivate a safe space where every individual can thrive and contribute their best.

That, in essence, is the blueprint for organizational success in the 21st century.

Designing for inclusiveness

Today, we are in an age of growing consciousness and increased awareness toward the neurodiverse spectrum, which encompasses conditions such as ADHD, Dyslexia, Autism, and other neurological conditions. Surprisingly, one in eight people is considered neurodivergent, yet fewer than 50% are aware of it. Neurodivergent individuals often demonstrate high energy, creative thinking, crisis management skills, and bold problem-solving abilities. However, they may encounter challenges when navigating the modern workplace. Designing inclusive workspaces is not only an ethical imperative but also makes for a strong business sense, motivating us to act for the greater good.

If you are enthusiastic about engaging with the younger generations who are increasingly self-aware, thanks to the efforts of Gen Xers and Millennials, it is essential to consider these aspects with greater depth. Anything designed to futureproof work environments should reflect the diverse makeup of organizations to ensure success for everyone.

But what does *"neurodivergent"* really mean?

The term "neurodivergent" refers to conditions such as autism spectrum disorder (ASD), attention deficit hyperactivity disorder (ADHD), Dyslexia, etc. Up to 17% of the population has been diagnosed with one or the other neurodivergent condition, such as:

- ADD/ADHD: 4%
- Autism: 1%
- Dyslexia: 10%
- Dyspraxia: 1%
- Tourette Syndrome: 1%

It's crucial to understand that the 17% figure is likely a conservative estimate, as many conditions go undiagnosed. The World Health Organization has identified the prevalence of neurological conditions as one of the greatest public health challenges, underscoring the need for increased awareness and understanding.

It's inspiring to see several forward-thinking industry leaders, including Microsoft, Amazon, Ford, JPMorgan Chase, EY, DXC Technology, Costco, and Google, investing in neurodiversity-at-work programs. Their efforts are not only commendable but also a source of hope for a more inclusive future. For instance, enterprise software firm SAP has set a goal to have 1% of its workforce comprised of individuals on the autistic spectrum by 2020, mirroring the global autistic population percentage. While SAP may not have reached the specific 1% goal mentioned, the company has made significant progress. SAP aimed to hire 650 employees on the autism spectrum when the program was launched (based on approximately 65,000 employees at the time); the latest information I could access suggested that SAP provided more than 800 opportunities for autistic individuals at various career stages.

Dyspraxia, Dyslexia, and Dyscalculia

Dyspraxia, also known as Developmental Coordination Disorder (DCD), is a complex neurological condition that affects multiple brain functions responsible for muscle coordination, perception, language, and thought. Individuals with dyspraxia often excel in creativity and innovative thinking, skills that can be strategically applied to solving complex workplace problems. Many entrepreneurs — such as Richard Branson, who has dyslexia, find that their condition helps them think creatively and find unique solutions.

Tourette Syndrome

Tourette Syndrome (TS) is a hereditary neurological condition characterized by involuntary tics, which can be physical (ranging from minor movements to major body motions) or verbal (such as laughing, talking, or coughing).

Parkinson's Disease Dementia

Parkinson's disease (PD) is the fastest-growing neurological disorder worldwide, and PD Dementia is dementia that's associated with PD. It is a progressive condition that affects dopamine-producing brain cells, which control movement, gradually causing loss of memory or impaired judgment. While the disease typically affects individuals over 50, it can be diagnosed as early as 20. Due to its slow progression, many individuals continue to have productive years post-diagnosis. However, as the workforce ages and retirement ages rise, addressing Parkinson's in the workplace is becoming increasingly important.

Comorbidity

Comorbidity, the coexistence of multiple conditions, is common among the neurodivergent population. For instance, two-thirds of individuals with ADD or ADHD have at least one other condition, such as Anxiety (34%), Depression (29%), Bipolar Disorder (12%), Substance Abuse (5-40%), Tourette Disorder (11%), Obsessive-Compulsive Disorder (4%), Oppositional Defiant Disorder (54-67%), or Conduct Disorder (22-43%).

It's essential to consider the rising prevalence of mental health conditions in our design process. Depression and anxiety, though not neurological disorders, are major mental health challenges in today's workplace. One in four people is likely to experience a mental health challenge at some point in their life, with stress being the most common. Stress often results from a combination of work, home, and personal factors. Ironically, despite the prevailing stigma, people are generally more open to discussing mental health than neurodiversity. Incorporating mental health considerations into workplace design is crucial for fostering an inclusive and supportive environment. This involves creating spaces that reduce stress and promote well-being, which can significantly enhance productivity and employee satisfaction.

Let's look at the Challenges Neurodivergent Individuals Face in the workplace.

Distractions:
- **Noise:** Acoustical distractions are a significant concern for over two-thirds of employees. Intermittent and unpredictable noises are particularly stressful, leading to a loss of productivity. Ironically, overly quiet offices can be just as distracting. The lack of background noise means that conversations and sounds from across the room are clearly audible, which can be highly disruptive.
- **Technology:** Constant notifications from phones, instant messages, and other communication tools can be more distracting than environmental noise.

Solutions for Distractions:
- Design spaces with diverse options, including areas designated for focus and concentration.
- Create tech-free zones to minimize the impact of constant digital interruptions.

Sensory Stimulation:
- Sensory cues can be overwhelming for individuals with developmental disabilities. It's important to have spaces where sensory stimulation can be controlled. The needs vary; some require more stimulation, while others are easily overwhelmed by it.

Wayfinding:
- Neurodivergent individuals often need repetition, predictability, and clear boundaries to feel safe and in control. Effective wayfinding is essential to make environments understandable.

- Spaces should not be overly redundant as they can lack inspiration. Designing areas with clear lines of sight, internal staircases, mezzanines, and memorable landmarks (through lighting, signage, art, and strategic use of color) helps with orientation and engagement.

How can Design make a difference?

Impact of Design on Occupants:
- Thoughtfully designed spaces can significantly impact productivity, satisfaction, and overall well-being.
- Providing a variety of workspace types caters to different tasks and preferences, helping to remove barriers and improve workplace culture.

Principles for Inclusive Design:
- **Variety and Choice:** Offer different types of workspaces to suit various tasks and preferences.
- **Flexibility:** Incorporate flexible design elements that can be adapted to individual needs, including areas for focused work, collaboration, and relaxation.
- **Sensory Considerations:** Create environments where sensory inputs can be controlled. This includes managing noise levels, lighting, and visual stimuli.
- **Intuitive Wayfinding:** Design spaces that are easy to navigate with clear signage, consistent layout, and visual cues to aid orientation.
- **Tech-Free Zones:** Implement areas where employees can disconnect from technology to reduce digital distractions.
- **Ergonomics and Comfort:** Ensure workstations are ergonomically designed to support physical well-being.

By addressing these challenges through thoughtful design, workplaces can become more inclusive, allowing neurodivergent individuals to thrive alongside their neurotypical colleagues.

- To create truly inclusive workspaces, the first step is conducting a thorough workplace assessment to pinpoint areas that may not fully support neurodivergent employees. This evaluation should involve gathering direct input from employees, especially those who are neurodivergent, to understand their specific needs and challenges. Armed with these insights, the next step is to design and plan workspaces that accommodate a diverse range of work styles, personality types, and abilities. This might involve creating quiet zones, collaborative areas, and relaxation spaces, ensuring that every employee has a setting that suits their needs. Importantly, most workplace adjustments are simple and affordable, with 95% of accommodations costing nothing for the employer.
- Raising awareness and educating the workforce about neurodiversity is also crucial. Implementing awareness and sensitivity programs can help neurotypical employees better understand and work alongside neurodivergent colleagues, appreciating their unique strengths and behaviors. Additionally, specific training should be offered to help employees adapt to or ignore certain neurodivergent behaviors, reducing potential misunderstandings and fostering a more inclusive and harmonious workplace environment.
- Environmental factors such as noise levels, lighting, and layout play a significant role in creating a comfortable workspace. Designing spaces that can be easily adjusted to meet individual sensory needs is essential. For instance, providing adjustable lighting, noise-canceling areas, and tech-free zones can help minimize distractions and enhance focus. Flexibility in design is key, allowing employees to choose the environment that best suits their current task and personal comfort.
- Investing in ergonomic furniture is another important aspect, ensuring that workstations are not only comfortable but also

supportive, which can reduce physical strain and promote better overall well-being. Effective wayfinding is also essential; clear signage, consistent layouts, and visual cues such as color coding and artwork can help everyone, particularly neurodivergent individuals, navigate the workplace with ease.

- Finally, fostering a culture of open communication is vital. Employees should feel comfortable discussing their needs and suggesting improvements. This can be facilitated through regular feedback sessions, anonymous surveys, and maintaining an open-door policy. It's also important to regularly review and update workplace policies to ensure they remain inclusive and supportive. This includes revisiting accommodation processes, flexible working arrangements, and mental health support services to ensure they continue to meet the evolving needs of all employees.

By taking these steps, organizations can create a work environment where all employees, regardless of their neurological differences, can thrive and contribute to the success of the business. This approach not only unleashes new opportunities but also fulfills a social and moral imperative to support diversity and inclusion.

After all, the future is going to be inclusive or nothing.

Workspace-as-a-Service

Recently, I was discussing the subject of future workspace with an academician friend when he brought forward an important point: over the past twenty years, there has been significant enthusiasm about the potential of technology to revolutionize the learning process. Advances in educational technology, particularly the use of AI and VR/AR, have greatly expanded the tools available for both students and educators to acquire new skills. Online platforms and customized learning programs have dramatically improved global access to knowledge. Additionally, the pandemic significantly accelerated the adoption of online learning, propelling the rapid growth of equitable education. Now, think about the actual impact of this? You could perhaps learn any technology that can fetch you a job from one of the platforms or even portals like YouTube. In other words, we are going to have a workforce capable of 'Do-it-yourself.' I am pretty sure GenZ would have never thought about a time when their older counterparts would have reached out to a travel agent to plan a trip. In the near future, homeschooling and online degrees will become totally acceptable for corporations if it isn't already.

What would really happen if GenZ and Gen Alpha, with a strong DIY culture, showed up at work?

One positive aspect is that they would likely be very independent and self-reliant. However, it's important to be aware that millennials and older colleagues might advocate for team-building and collaboration.

Imagine a scenario where a younger team is working on a project and prefers to handle it entirely on their own, possibly achieving better results that way. Their manager, who has a millennial perspective, might naturally feel that allowing the project to run independently without frequent check-ins could be risky. It's understandable—many of us instinctively believe that two or more minds collaborating are better than one.

The solution to this challenge lies in millennials and older generations becoming more adept at handing off responsibilities to their younger colleagues while establishing clear ground rules for regular check-ins. This approach could lead to a shift from long collaboration sessions to shorter, more focused check-ins. Consequently, this might influence how we design collaboration spaces, meeting rooms, and even small community work environments where young teams interact with their managers. While there isn't a one-size-fits-all answer, it's essential to carefully analyze these dynamics and craft workspaces that are tailored to the team's size, the nature of their work, and their daily interactions.

Another important aspect to be mindful of is the rise of the freelance economy. After Wipro terminated 300 employees for allegedly "working for rival companies" while still on its payroll, moonlighting became a hot topic, sparking a wave of memes, posts, and opinions across social media. The issue has divided employees and employers into two camps: one views moonlighting as unethical and illegal, while the other defends it as a financial necessity. Although the concept is controversial and has sparked significant debate, there is no explicit law against moonlighting within the Indian constitutional framework. The more I discussed this issue with people, the more I sensed that moonlighting is becoming increasingly popular, especially among the younger generation who have recently entered the workforce and face financial anxiety in a "competitive, ruthless, and under-equipped" corporate environment. A survey found that 64% of full-time Gen Z workers are interested in participating in the gig economy, and 37% would consider changing employers if they are not allowed to moonlight.

While the exact figure of 64% of full-time Gen Z workers interested in the gig economy is not directly supported by the given search results, there is evidence of significant interest:

- According to a 2023 Deloitte report, 46% of Gen Z workers in the U.S. are already participating in the gig economy
- A 2022 study by Upwork found that 43% of Gen Z workers have performed freelance work

These figures suggest a strong interest in gig work among Gen Z, though the percentage is lower than the 64% mentioned in the survey.

Before dismissing these youngsters as naive or lazy, it's essential to understand the thought process behind their choices. When most of us imagine starting a business, we picture the classic startup entrepreneur—someone who made it big after countless investor pitches and assembling a wide range of resources. However, from a Gen Z perspective, starting a business often means something entirely different. They frequently envision a one-person operation, which we might refer to as freelancing, but they see themselves as true business owners. This shift in mindset reflects their desire for independence and control over their work, which they view as entrepreneurship in its own form. One of the recent research studies I looked at found that, from Q1 to Q2 in 2020, the number of freelancers in India jumped by 46%. There are approximately 15 million freelancers in India. It is beginning to become a large workforce.

Now the big question is, in the future age of talent war, if you are someone who is keenly looking for the right talent on the table, could you ignore them?

Upwork in the US is a great example of a company that brings these two groups together for potential business opportunities. It's a work marketplace that connects businesses with independent professionals or freelancers, offering companies greater flexibility while providing freelancers with more opportunities. This model could inspire the design of future workspaces, allowing for a more fluid blend of traditional employees and independent workers. If this trend continues, future offices might need to incorporate areas that can seamlessly integrate these teams with full-time employees. At the very least, workplaces should have the flexibility to adapt to such changes.

As we look to the future, with the youngest generations dominating the workspace, reimagining office spaces as operational expenses rather than capital investments is going to emerge as a key trend. This shift is poised to transform how businesses support the increasingly agile, post-pandemic workforce. Organizations around the globe are already seeing significant benefits from this approach, including enhanced employee satisfaction and productivity, reduced costs associated with underutilized office space, and broader access to global talent.

Envisioning a workspace that evolves in tandem with your organization's needs offers exciting possibilities. Rather than waiting to accumulate capital for a major redesign or relocation, businesses can now adapt their offices to meet current requirements and future demands. This involves overhauling traditional financial models and redesigning office environments to boost employee well-being and efficiency. By incorporating elements from various working models—such as traditional, co-working, core and flex, hybrid, and remote workspaces—companies can create versatile, functional, and aesthetically pleasing environments.

In this, businesses will focus on the perfect blend of design, layout, location, psychological impact, and technology, supported by a customized and sustainable financial model. The future of workspaces is not only about adapting but also about innovating to create the ideal environment for both present and future needs. Thinking about financing your workspace in this way is not just smart—it's essential for maintaining financial flexibility while investing in the future of your business; I am sure CFOs would love this design and office as a service you may be subscribing to!

Creating a true workplace experience

If I had to sum up what the future holds for the workplace, it would be the "workplace experience." This term encompasses everything an employee encounters in the now-limited time they spend in the office. In today's virtual and hybrid work environments, fostering employee engagement and human connection relies heavily on person-to-person interactions. For instance, consider the vibrant atmosphere of an in-person company all-hands meeting or a live concert. Now, imagine trying to replicate that experience by watching the same event on your computer. Even if you manage to avoid distractions and stay focused, the online experience falls short. In a remote work setting, the need for meaningful, direct interactions becomes crucial in enhancing employee experience, engagement, and loyalty. Let's break this down to explore opportunities for the workplaces of the future.

As part of my journey to understand how younger generations navigate workplace dynamics, I sat down with a recent graduate who had just entered the workforce. I asked him about his experience in making friends at his new job, and his response was quite telling. He shared, "Lately, I've been taking my work more seriously and have become more hesitant about forming close friendships at the office. Since I've only been with this company for a few months and work in a hybrid setup, it's been more challenging to build relationships with colleagues. It's not that I'm unwilling to connect with others, but after previously blurring the lines between professional and personal relationships, I now find it refreshing to keep some distance." This realization seems to align with a broader trend—work friendships are becoming less common, and the more I think about it, the more I believe this might be a positive shift.

This reminds me of the viral forwards you may have seen, which say, "There are no real friends at the workplace." One key reason behind the decline in work friendships is the rise of remote work. It's difficult to establish a strong connection with a colleague through networking tools like Slack and Zoom alone. While many white-collar employees are no longer fully remote, a significant number still work in hybrid environments, complicating the process of forming close workplace friendships.

The more I thought about it, the more I felt that for Gen Z, work and personal life are two distinct spheres, and the workplace is not necessarily seen as a place for socializing. Having entered the workforce during a time when remote work became the norm, many Gen Zers are unaccustomed to forming strong social connections with colleagues. The convenience of remote work often outweighs the sense of connectedness that in-office work provides. Despite widespread reports of loneliness among Gen Z, these feelings are not strong enough to push them toward building workplace friendships.

The absence of social connections at work is closely linked to Gen Z's high rates of job-hopping, as friendships and a sense of belonging are crucial factors in fostering commitment to a particular workplace. Workplaces often serve as a significant source of community, offering unofficial mentorship and networking opportunities that can greatly impact an employee's experience and growth.

These trends in workplace friendships are occurring alongside troubling statistics about poor mental health and high levels of loneliness in this generation. Whether these feelings of isolation will eventually lead Gen Z to seek out more in-person connections at the office remains to be seen.

They are quite clear about not buying into the "work is your family" rhetoric. Once communicated well, they understand that social interactions at work play a crucial role in influencing job performance. Feeling like a valued member of a team is not just about enjoying the work environment; it also enhances innovation, engagement, and the quality of work, as Simon and his team discovered. This sense of belonging is particularly important for individuals who may not have a large social circle outside of work.

From a workplace design perspective, this also influences how offices of the future might be shaped. Contrary to the much-discussed open collaboration and agility, there may be a need for personal spaces or "pit stops." Some employees expressed a strong desire for a personal desk—a home base where they can keep their belongings permanently. While they appreciate the collaborative nature of an open workspace, they also prefer having visual privacy to help them focus when needed. They value a variety of workspace options that cater to different work styles and tasks, whether it's individual work or team projects. Whether they're at home, in the office, at their desk, in a booth, or enjoying coffee in a lounge, they want the flexibility to choose the best environment for the task at hand. This approach reflects how many of us have adapted to working over the past couple of years, using different settings depending on the needs of the moment.

What Gen Z is teaching us is the importance of open dialogue, mutual respect, and trust in creating a supportive community that can unite everyone. They want to work with people who trust them to choose the work environment that allows them to deliver their best results. The good thing is, if you take a slightly different approach in your layout, keeping what we discussed in mind, it will work for everyone, not just younger generations.

Now, let's look at engaging with the brand. Understanding the power of branding can make all the difference in your competitive edge and your ability to attract the younger generation. Straightforward as it can get, although many believe that branding is limited to logos and websites, it runs much deeper. Branding is the essence of who you are, what you do, why you do it, how you do it, and who you do it for. When you get this right, it attracts the right talent and sets you apart, creating a strong sense of distinctiveness. The brand you create must resonate at every single 'touchpoint' for the employees. This can mean your logo and website, of course, but it also includes how your people talk about where they work and your office spaces. Your brand experience encompasses all the impressions and emotions your employees encounter when interacting with your brand across every touchpoint. It reflects the culmination of your brand promise, performance, and perception.

Gen Z is seeking more than just a job; they want a compelling reason to be part of a company. To secure their commitment, it's crucial to understand and address their values, individual needs, and personal beliefs. You need to be consistently attentive and responsive to what motivates your employees and how they perceive their workplace. This requires ongoing effort from management to stay attractive and aligned with the interests and values of their teams. A strong employer brand strategy is key to attracting and retaining top talent, and employee engagement is a big part of that equation. Workplace design can be seen as an important tool for enhancing and delivering this strategy.

As we conclude this book, I want to leave you with some unique insights from a distinguished industry leader, Mr. Tim Larson. Based in our Singapore studio, Mr. Larson is the Chief Creative Officer and Unispace Managing Director for Asia. With over 25 years of experience, he has been a leading innovator in designing emerging experiences and interactions within architectural environments. Previously the Design Principal at Downstream, our experience design agency, Mr. Larson pioneered new approaches in corporate interiors, retail stores, and sports and entertainment venues. In our insightful conversation, he shared crucial perspectives that are essential for you to understand.

As a technologist and futurist, how do you envision the office of the future? What key features or technologies do you believe will define this space?

The office of the future will be significantly shaped by major trends such as hybridization, downsized offices, and the de-influencing of work-from-home. These trends will pave the way for more employee-centric spaces, acknowledging the diverse ways of working and the need for well-being. The future office will feature new work points, including outdoor offices and a more relaxed environment. It will also be equipped with intelligent, AI-enabled work tech that simplifies, optimizes, and enhances the user experience, placing the employee at the center of the design process.

In what ways do you think workplaces will differ for Generation Z and Generation Alpha compared to previous generations? How will their expectations and working styles shape the future office environment?

Our data shows that Gen Z workers are more satisfied with current hybrid work models, and Gen Alpha is less satisfied. This means the evolution of the workplace will continue to meet the needs of a generation of workers who want even more flexibility and balance. Employees have a desire to feel proud of the places they work and share the same values, so workplaces need to mirror those values in things like DEI and ESG.

How should workplace designers and strategists approach the challenges and opportunities presented by a multigenerational workforce? Understanding and addressing the unique needs of different age groups is crucial. What strategies should be employed to ensure that these diverse needs are met?

There is a clear generational divide in the data that suggests older employees value time in the office and younger employees value more work flexibility. Balancing the design to cater to both these preferences is a complex but critical task. Older workers come to the office to focus, and younger workers value social interaction. Providing privacy and focus areas alongside collaborative and social/communal spaces is attractive to both groups in different ways. Younger employees are attracted to things like huddle spaces and collaboration rooms, and older employees like private and semi-private spaces, so providing this balance is critical.

What significant changes do you foresee happening in the workplace? Is there a particular trend or innovation that you believe will have a transformative impact on how we work?

Flexibility and adaptation continue to be the key drivers. The workplace of the future will be a collection of different types of environments and non-traditional work points. Occupancy data, sensors, and AI-enabled work tech will help us optimize and improve the employee experience in real time. The workplace will continue to evolve and become places that are social hubs, spaces for spontaneous interaction and emotional connection. Successful organizations will craft casual, community-focused havens that cultivate a sense of belonging and unity, drawing people together over shared experience, values, and success and thereby winning the hearts, minds, and loyalty of employees over the long term.

CONCLUSION

As we conclude our beautiful exploration of workplace dynamics and adaptive designs, let's envision a wonderful future where every workspace will be a hub of creativity, collaboration, and well-being. By incorporating the principles outlined in this book into your work culture, you can easily create a platform where individuals from diverse backgrounds and generations not only coexist but thrive.

Throughout this exploration, we've traversed the diverse landscape of the modern workforce, where multiple generations converge, each with their own unique perspectives, preferences, and expectations. We've witnessed the evolving nature of work itself, propelled by technological advancements, shifting societal norms, and an increasingly interconnected global economy.

Remember, the journey to designing an adaptive workplace is a continuous process. It requires constant sanding and sculpting. I'm sure this book has helped you learn, adapt, and commit to putting people at the center of your design decisions. With each step forward, we inch closer to a future where work is not just a place we go but a space where we feel inspired, supported, and valued. Employees hate Mondays as they are fully aware of the hectic workload that they might be entrusted with. On Sundays, they probably sit and curse the upcoming week. You can bring a change to this situation by providing a lovely open space where your employees can spend some time. This will help them prevent burnout, and they will no longer go to bed depressed on a Sunday night or stay grumpy throughout the week.

The path to designing an adaptive workplace is not without its challenges. It requires the courage to challenge conventional wisdom, to question established norms, and to embrace uncertainty as an opportunity for growth. It calls for a pragmatic approach that considers not only the physical aspects of the workspace but also the social, emotional, and psychological dimensions of the human experience.

So, let's together create a splendid future—a future where every workplace is as dynamic and vibrant as the people who inhabit it, a future of never-ending creativity, collaboration, and everything else that will keep everyone happy!

As we navigate through this journey together, we must remain observant in our pursuit of excellence, cognizant of the evolving needs and aspirations of the individuals we serve. We must cultivate a culture of inclusivity and diversity, where every voice is heard and every perspective is valued. We must foster a sense of belonging and community, where individuals feel empowered to express themselves authentically and to connect with others on a deeper level.

In raising our glasses to the future of work, let us toast to the boundless potential that lies within each and every one of us. Let us celebrate the spirit of innovation, the power of collaboration, and the joy of discovery and embrace the challenges that lie ahead with courage and conviction, knowing that together, we can build a better tomorrow—one workspace at a time.

So, as we bid farewell to these pages, let us carry forward with us the lessons learned and the insights gained as we continue to shape the future of work for generations to come. Cheers to a future filled with promise, purpose, and endless opportunity.

REFERENCES

1. Slide, Jacob. "Challenging Perceptions: Exploring Actual vs Perceived Inter & Intra Generational Differences in Values Placed on Work-Related Concepts Conducted During Covid 19 BY Jacob Slide," 2023. *https://digitalcommons.bryant.edu/cgi/viewcontent.cgi?article=1047&context=honors_management.*
2. "TiVo, Bengaluru." M Moser Associates, November 21, 2023. *https://www.mmoser.com/projects/tivo-bengaluru/.*
3. McLaurin, Janet Pogue. "Younger Generations Work Differently. What Does This Mean for the Future Workplace?" Gensler, May 17, 2023. *https://www.gensler.com/blog/younger-generations-work-differently-future-workplace.*
4. "Bottomline." Unispace. Accessed August 30, 2024. *https://www.unispace.com/projects/bottomline_india.*
5. "Digitising an Innovative Scalable Workplace; Citi Office Design, Chennai." M Moser Associates, July 18, 2024. *https://www.mmoser.com/projects/citi-chennai/.*
6. Unispace. "Re:Location: Co-Working and Flexibility: Keeping Your Business Goals in Mind." Unispace. Accessed August 30, 2024.

https://www.unispace.com/insights/relocation-co-working-and-flexibility.

7. Joy, Andrew, and Barry P. Haynes. "Office Design for the Multi-Generational Knowledge Workforce." Journal of Corporate Real Estate 13, no. 4 (November 22, 2011): 216–32.
https://doi.org/10.1108/14630011111214428.

8. Dr. Borne, Bea. "Generational Differences in the Workplace [Infographic]." Purdue Global. Accessed August 30, 2024.
https://www.purdueglobal.edu/education-partnerships/generational-workforcedifferences-infographic/

9. Ahmadi, Matthew N, Pieter Coenen, Leon Straker, and Emmanuel Stamatakis. "Device-Measured Stationary Behaviour and Cardiovascular and Orthostatic Circulatory Disease Incidence." OUP Academic, October 16, 2024.
https://academic.oup.com/ije/article/53/6/dyae136/7822310.

10. "Digital Nomad Statistics You Should Know 2024." Pumble Learn, April 22, 2024.
https://pumble.com/learn/digital-nomad-visa/statistics/.

www.ingramcontent.com/pod-product-compliance
Lightning Source LLC
LaVergne TN
LVHW011420080426
835512LV00005B/176